Stones of Remembrance

Compiled by Chaplin
Cindy L. McKinley

Unless otherwise indicated, all Scripture quotations are from The Authorized (King James) Version. Rights in the Authorized Version in the United Kingdom are vested in the Crown. Reproduced by permission of the Crown's patentee, Cambridge University Press

Copyright © 2022 Cindy L. McKinley
All rights reserved.
ISBN- 9798826205426

A Note from Cindy
More Than Conquerors Director

The purpose of the *More Than Conquerors* ministry is to build a supportive community that will help our widows and widowers stay connected with our Ministry Network and with others who are walking this same journey.

We all have a story to tell and we can learn from those who are willing to share their story.

Our Stones of Remembrance contains stories written by the widows and widowers of credential holders in the Pennsylvania/Delaware Ministry Network of the Assemblies of God. Their lives were drastically changed with the passing of their spouse.

It is our prayer that you will be blessed and encouraged as you read the stories shared in this book.

This Book is Dedicated to:

A very special group of people in my life, the *More Than Conquerors* (MTC) of the Pennsylvania/Delaware Ministry Network of the Assemblies of God.

In one breath your life was turned upside down. You quickly found yourself on a new and uninvited journey. Your willingness to share bits and pieces of your lives is what made *Our Stones of Remembrance* possible.

I cherish the times we have spent together either in person or via phone conversations. Your heart and passion for serving God, even in the darkest hours, have ministered to me deeply throughout the years.

                Never Forget You Are Dearly Loved!

A Thankful Heart

First and foremost, I give thanks to my Lord Jesus Christ. He is the reason you are holding this book in your hands today. Over the years I have learned, that His timing is perfect and without Him, I can do nothing!

To my amazing husband Robin. Throughout our forty-three years of marriage, you have been my biggest supporter. Many times you have gently pushed me past my comfort zone. You have always seen a greater potential within me than I could see. Your encouragement has enabled me to take each step toward something bigger than myself, even if it meant cooking dinner, doing laundry and so much more. Robin, I could have never accomplished all that I have if you weren't there cheering me on. Thank you for all the hours you spent supporting and helping me put this book together.

To my children Chris, Amanda, Jonathan, and Mandi. Your encouragement and support bless my heart. You have been so patient with me when my schedule gets a little crazy.

Acknowledgements

Dr. Donald J. Immel, the Superintendent of the Pennsylvania/Delaware Ministry Network of the Assemblies of God. Your support for this vital ministry is what makes projects like this happen. Your love and concern for our *More Than Conquerors* are shown by all you do in ministering to our widows and widowers.

The following people have been an awesome support team:

My proofreaders:
Jarusha Bonitz, Kathy Caruso, Vivian Dippold, Linda Doell, Rhonda Imes, Susan Lanza, Florence Whittaker

The artwork:
Pamela Matak of "Pamela's Heart." Check out her website at **PamelasHeart.com**.

Cover Design:
A special thanks to my son Jonathan McKinley. He always amazed me with his God-given gifts and talents.

Celeste Falvo whom God has used to springboard me into a much broader ministry to widows and widowers.

God Bless You All
Cindy

History of More Than Conquerors Ministry
Marlene Martin

During a very difficult time in your life, have you ever experienced the Lord giving you a promise of an answer? The promise was so sure that it burned in your soul. It could be a promise of salvation of a loved one or owning a home, or even something that you feel would never come to pass. But, deep in your heart, God had spoken and said, "I will answer."

In my case, I had this burden upon my heart for a very special group of people. It would overwhelm me at times and the only person I would talk to about it was my husband. He'd encourage me to pray and seek the Lord for His direction.

In August of 1993, my husband had to go to Springfield, MO, on a business trip. As we were sitting and talking in the restaurant, Brother and Sister Grove came walking in. Jayne Grove was the Women's Director of the PennDel District at that time. We sat and shared a wonderful time of fellowship and then went our separate ways.

About two weeks went by and I received a letter from Sister Grove. In it, she stated that while we were in Springfield having lunch, the Lord kept prompting her to ask me a question. She said she kept saying to the Lord, "Why should I ask Marlene?" She shrugged it off, but ever since that day, the Lord had not let her rest. Now she was writing to ask me, "Would I consider and pray about a particular ministry?"

I couldn't believe what I was reading. What was the ministry? It was the need to reach out to pastors' wives who have lost their husbands and to pastors who have lost their wives. This was the very burden the Lord had placed on my heart over fifteen years prior.

I had a big task ahead of me since there were no records of who our widows and widowers were. I began contacting the mature pastors and their wives, asking them to help me with this list. It was a long hard task, but we got it organized. The letters I received from these precious people would have broken your hearts. I knew, without a doubt, that this is what God wanted me to do for our District.

I headed up this ministry for over nineteen years. Most of these people I had never met but talking with them and writing letters made us a real family. Eventually, I felt that it was important to make a list of our retirees. They could be another group that could reach out to them.

Two years before I stepped down, I knew God was speaking to me once again as to who was to take the reins. She was a dedicated pastor's wife and served as the Women's Representative for the East Central Section. She was one of my biggest supporters. I knew whom to ask. I couldn't just blurt it out, but I knew with great confidence it would be Cindy McKinley. She's a pastor's wife, mother, grandmother and a woman who has worked hard at what God has called her to accomplish. She has become Ordained through the Assemblies of God and her passion for this ministry is very evident.

I'm thankful for the PennDel Ministry Network for standing behind this vital ministry and I'm so proud of Cindy, a true woman of God.

I thank God that I had a small part in accomplishing what God had in mind for His special group of people. He has a lot of "special groups of people" and He needs someone to fill in the gap. Could He be speaking to you about a "special" group? Allow Him to direct your steps.

"...The Lord said to Joshua, "Now choose twelve men, one from each tribe. Tell them, 'Take twelve stones from the very place where the priests are standing in the middle of the Jordan. Carry them out and pile them up at the place where you will camp tonight.'"

So Joshua called together the twelve men he had chosen...He told them, "Go into the middle of the Jordan, in front of the Ark of the Lord your God. Each of you must pick up one stone and carry it out on your shoulder...We will use these stones to build a memorial. In the future, your children will ask you, 'What do these stones mean?' Then you can tell them, 'They remind us that the Jordan River stopped flowing when the Ark of the Lord's Covenant went across.' These stones will stand as a memorial among the people of Israel forever."

- Joshua 4:1-7 (NLT)

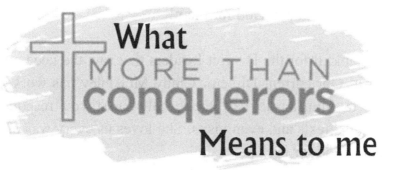

Dear Friends,

This is what *More Than Conquerors* has meant to me - like-mindedness!

This group understands not only the enormous grief of losing the love of my life but also losing the ministry we had together. Sharing their journey helped in my healing. Hearing their stories and what they were doing for the Lord alone gave me HOPE. Sharing about their families showed me Healing! I know I'm not alone in this crazy Grief Journey! Mentoring is an amazing gift! Thank God for them!

I am so thankful for the District Leaders that saw the need and acted on it. Our current Director Cindy McKinley has worked tirelessly to minister to us! Phone calls until you respond, cards, emails, texts and even visits. She loves us every way she can! Thank God for her!

May this ministry continue to bless and encourage!

United In Christ!
- Celeste Falvo

The *More Than Conquerors* ministry has been a tremendous encouragement since my husband's heavenly home-going. The quarterly newsletters, the personal phone calls from Cindy, and the special birthday and Christmas cards with special gifts are wonderful reminders that we are still appreciated and loved.

Cindy is truly called to minister to us with her compassion, her sincere love and concern, and all her prayers for the ever-growing list of widows and widowers.

God bless her ABUNDANTLY for leading the *More Than Conquerors* ministry for the PennDel Ministry Network.

- Marilyn Evans

Thank God for the *More Than Conquerors* ministry. He has been so faithful! I read the emails, newsletters and cards over and over. I'm thankful for all the Pennsylvania-Delaware Ministry Network of the Assemblies of God does for widows and widowers. I so appreciate each of them and my prayer is that God will continue to bless and keep them.

- Rev. Alex Velazquez, Jr.

The *More Than Conquerors* ministry is one of the Assemblies of God's best-kept secrets. That is because it is targeted to an exclusive group of people who have had the honor of working in ministry and now are on an unexpected/expected life journey…they are widows and widowers.

The *More Than Conquerors* is led by a compassionate, sensitive leader named Cindy McKinley. Cindy has a special God-given passion for those going through this grieving process.

My husband Abe Oliver was promoted into the Lord's presence seven and a half years ago.

After more than fifty years of serving by his side in ministry, I found myself not only in a state of grief but, as time went by, feeling isolated and anonymous. That journey's description is for another time. What I did find was faithful birthday and Christmas cards, in addition to quarterly newsletters, received from *More Than Conquerors*. This encouraged me in trying to adjust to my "new normal." I am grateful to Cindy and our District Superintendent Dr. Donald Immel for seeing the value that still exists in those whose positions have changed but whose passion to serve the Lord has not.

- Nilli Oliver

The *More Than Conquerors* are a blessing to me and my daughter. It has been good to know there are folks out there that are praying and thinking of you. Sometimes it seems you are all alone with no one to turn to or no one cares, but you know the *More Than Conquerors* do, for they have shown it many times over the years. Cindy and the *More Than Conqueror*s make sure you feel you are loved and prayed for. They are a true blessing. I thank God for them.

- Darlene Fulton

I've been a *More Than Conqueror* since 2018. Our *MTC* Director Cindy McKinley has a heart of compassion for her ministry to each of us widows and widowers. The quarterly newsletter gives us a birds-eye glimpse into the lives of others, just like me. She ministers personally with periodic phone calls and prayer.

When my heart is crying inside, *More Than Conquerors* is an encouragement and reminder of who God intends me to be…a *More Than Conqueror*. To me, the Master Designer of this ministry is God. *More Than Conquerors* is an extension of His arms and hands to deliver hugs where needed through encouragement, and an opportunity to pray for the needs of others who are experiencing the same journey as you. *More Than Conquerors* is a lifeline that I am so grateful to receive. It brings so clearly into focus Psalm 68:5 *"Father of orphans and protector of widows is God in His holy habitation."*

- Barbara Stigile

I am so blessed to be a part of *More than Conquerors*. Our leader, Pastor Cindy, cares for us so deeply. She keeps us informed through her quarterly newsletters, phone calls and emails. She encourages us and prays for us. I am so blessed by her ministry. The quarterly newsletters are done with such beauty and excellence, and they are so informative. It is so good to be able to share our joys, sorrows and health problems so we know better how to pray for each other. I especially enjoy all the pictures in each newsletter.

When there is an urgent prayer request, we are notified by email. Pastor Cindy also calls or emails us to inquire about the person or situation that needed prayer.

The fellowship we enjoy at our annual District Council meeting and other special times is wonderful. It's a good way to stay connected with one another.

Another way that helps us stay connected is by the quarterly list of names, addresses, birthdays and phone numbers. This is a real help!

Probably the greatest reason I'm glad to be a part of *More Than Conquerors* is for the encouragement I receive, as well as the opportunity to reach out to others.

- Ruby Mayeski

He was only seventy-seven when he died suddenly of cardiac arrest in 2019. It was one day before our fifty-fifth wedding anniversary. John Q. Kenzy was the love of my life. We went to work in Brooklyn Teen Challenge, arriving one week after we were married. We were in active ministry at the time of his death. To say I was shocked is an understatement.

John was licensed and ordained in the New York District of the Assemblies of God and transferred his credentials to the Pennsylvania Delaware Ministry Network in 1973.

I didn't know there was an outreach to widows/widowers until I got a phone call from Cindy McKinley, whom I had not met. I felt her warm embrace and love over the phone as she began to tell me about this vital ministry. Her expression of condolences and prayer are amazing. Though I have yet to meet Cindy, I feel like she is a dear friend (because she is). She is a compassionate and caring Director of the vital ministry of *More Than Conquerors* (MTC). What a treasure she is!

This ministry has been timely and so encouraging for those of us who may struggle with the title of "widow." My faith is firm; my heart is focused on Jesus but having a partner in faith at such a time as this is surely a gift from God. I am SO thankful for the Network's awareness of such a need -- even though I never dreamed I would be a recipient of their love and encouragement.

Thank you, Cindy McKinley, and the Pennsylvania-Delaware Ministry Network for this vital outreach to the bereaved, being there whenever needed.

- Carol Kenzy, a graduate of Evangel University in 1964
(John Q. Kenzy, graduate of Central Bible College in 1964)
MTC recipient since June 2019

My heart has been touched and greatly moved by these personal experiences. Many of these experiences, I have been through while serving with my husband in forty-eight years of ministry. The tears welled up as the impact of each anecdote and the emotionally moving thoughts touched the depth of my spirit. After reading these, I have found a newness of gratitude for the blessings of years gone by. God has not changed through the generations.

We, as the older population, now have the responsibility to build the altars of remembrance. We need to churn the memories of old-time Pentecost and share the stories of having limited (or many times – non-existent) finances. We need to demonstrate to this younger generation of Shepherds that Jesus never fails. These submissions will indeed do just that!

I want to say a personal "Thank you" and a big "air" hug to those More Than Conqueror Partners who so willingly opened their hearts to share the funny but sometimes distressing memories. I have found a common thread ringing through all the articles. God is our Compass. God is our Guide. God is the Healer. God is the Provider. God is the Comfort to the Lonely.

Praising Jesus for the faithfulness of those He has CALLED.

~ Vivian Dippold (Husband – Otto Dippold - 10/18/18)

Memories from the Hills of West Virginia
Bonnie Linton

I became a Christian in August 1948. Years later I met my husband at a youth camp in the Potomac District. We were both playing the accordion.

For several years, before we were married, I had a bad kidney problem. I would be in and out of the hospital two or three times a month. After we were married, the doctors were very concerned about what would happen when I would be pregnant. We prayed about it and I never had any more problems. I delivered a healthy, 9 lb. 14 oz., baby boy and never had a problem since.

We answered God's call on our lives, and our first church was in Mathias in the mountains of West Virginia. We were warned that there were certain roads in the mountains that we were not safe to drive on. Those roads led to the "moonshine" stills. If the owners saw someone they didn't know on those roads, they were prepared to shoot!

God always provided for us. We got a call one day that a lady from the church was very ill in the Winchester Hospital. The car needed gas and we didn't have money, so we weren't able to go. That day, I decided to clean the bedroom closet. I took down an old purse and decided to throw it away. I opened it to see if anything was inside. There was a $20 bill. God had to put it there. In those times, I never remember having $20, much less putting it in a purse and hiding it!

While living in Mathias, and nine months pregnant, I went to my parents' house in Maryland, because we were a very long distance from the hospital. During that time, my husband was teaching in a one-room schoolhouse up in the mountains and this young girl came running into the school. She told my husband that he would have to come and take her sister to the mountain clinic because she was already having a baby. When my husband got there, it was too late, the baby had already been born. So, he had to help! He called the nurse at the clinic, but she couldn't come because she was also delivering a baby at the clinic. She would help him by talking him through it on the phone. There was terrible phone service and my husband would ask the phone operator questions. She would ask the nurse and then give my husband the answer. He asked the girl's mother to boil some water because everything was filthy. The mother boiled the water to sterilize it, only to pour their cold water into it to cool it down! When he asked for Vaseline to put on the umbilical cord, she brought him bacon grease! The windows were broken and several stray dogs were standing around. The nurse arrived just as my husband was leaving.

Great Memories
Rev. *Angeline Antin*

I was raised in a Christian home but didn't start to serve the Lord until I was twenty-nine years old. How I met my husband is a long story, one of which we would share in many churches. He was my miracle. It was my nephew, Rev. Dale Everett, who introduced us. We are a blended family. I had three children and he had four. Many are still in the ministry.

My favorite Bible verse is *"Wait for the Lord; be strong, and let your heart be courageous. Wait for the Lord."* Psalm 27:14 (CSB)

A funny story for my husband and me was when the people of the church wanted him to play his violin, while I accompanied him. I started on what I thought was the right key and he started on the wrong key. Everyone laughed. But, of course, I got in HIS key and it all turned out well.

I have served in the PennDel District and taught an adult class in Enola, PA, played the piano, and led a ladies' prayer meeting. In Niagara Falls, I taught a new convert's class. I stayed very busy for the Lord.

Note: *Angie spent her final days in a nursing home. Although not happy about her circumstances, she decided to let her light shine for Jesus. In her short time there, Angie prayed for the residents and staff. Many staff members would come to her room on their break because they felt so much peace there. With great excitement, she said, "I just let my light shine and Jesus does the rest!" Angie touched their lives in such a profound way. She was asked to start a Bible study and taught one class before she when home to be with Jesus.*

Learning to Lean
Lorraine Swank

My husband Jim and I attended EBI (Eastern Bible Institute/the University of Valley Forge) six months after we were married. During Jim's last semester, EBI President Well asked Jim to consider pastoring Maranatha Assembly of God in Lansdale, PA, just about thirty minutes away from the Bible School.

Jim became pastor in January 1954 and we stayed on campus until he graduated in May. We spent the first five years of our ministry loving and caring for a precious fold who also loved and cared for us. It was both exciting and challenging. Many souls were saved during that time. The church moved the congregation from a storeroom to a renovated building at the edge of town. The congregation numbered well over 100.

We learned valuable lessons and saw our great God move in His own awesome way. The church was not able to pay us very much, but we experienced the faithful provision of God…over and over again! Our daughter Kerri was born while we attended EBI/UVF, and our son Glenn was born when we were in Lansdale.

Many Great Memories
Rev. Sylvia Baker

As a young girl, I attended Sunday School at the nearby Methodist Church in Swissvale, a suburb of Pittsburgh. I went with a couple of girlfriends. Although I learned about God and Jesus and enjoyed being in Sunday School, my first introduction to evangelical Christianity was during Billy Graham's Pittsburgh Crusade in 1952. I went forward and was ministered to by their staff. I attended and raised my children in the Presbyterian Church, but my real encounter with Jesus occurred through the Charismatic Movement that literally blew through Pittsburgh in the early 1970s. As a result of my teenage daughters attending a Russ Bixler prayer and praise service, I, too, went to the meetings and ultimately gave my heart to Jesus one very late night - 1:30 a.m. on July 23, 1971. A few weeks later, as I was driving through the Squirrel Hill Tunnels on an errand for my boss, I asked for and received the baptism in the Holy Spirit, right there in the car. About three years later, my husband, too, recommitted his life and also received the baptism, which led our family to an Assembly of God church. And the rest is history…as they say!

My passion in high school was roller skating. Every night the rink was open, I was there. A young man, who I greatly enjoyed skating with, wasn't there for a few nights. When he finally came back, he invited me to my first Billy Graham Crusade meeting, which I then attended every night for about a month. My girlfriends insisted one Saturday night near the end of the Crusade that I go skating with them.

As it happened, this very handsome soldier named Roy Baker showed up and asked me to skate with him. At the end of the evening, he asked if he could take me home. I said, "Yes, but only if we walked." What he didn't know was that home was about six miles away. We did just that and six months later we were married. We were married for 40 years until his early death in 1993.

Upon receiving my first set of credentials in 1996, my pastor at Pitcairn Assembly of God asked if I would consider coming on staff with him as Assistant Pastor to which I happily agreed. Since Pitcairn was my home church, there were some unique circumstances. Nevertheless, I was accepted and blessed by both the "old-timers" and the "newcomers." I served with Pastor Dave Scolforo for three years. Upon his resignation, I, too, resigned in July 1999. Two months later, I was invited to begin my tenure with Shanksville Assembly of God.

There's always room for a good laugh and that came when I was introduced to another pastor as Sylvia Baker. He promptly asked, "Are you married to Moses?" A bit shocked, I replied, "I'm not THAT old." With a bit of embarrassment, he stated that he knew a Pastor Moses Baker.

For years I have enjoyed running and walking 5K and 10K races and have participated in Somerset, Pittsburgh and Ligonier runs. I started running and found it a good time for praying, thinking and enjoying the beautiful countryside. I came in first place in many of my races, mostly because I was the only one in my age division.

I am so thankful He never gave up on me and will never leave me alone.

Miracles: Experienced & Unexpected
Rev. Betty Swank

A miracle always has a beginning. We had a used car when my husband went to be with the Lord. I continued to drive it well after John was gone but, as we all know, cars do need to have repairs. I made the appointment. Soon the repairman called to say the car needed certain repairs, but the price would be expensive. The repairs would be more than the car was worth, so I decided to keep it for parts.

The town we lived in had a free bus service for senior citizens. When I had to go to the store to buy groceries, I called for the bus to drive to the house, because that was all I really needed for transportation. Anywhere else, I could walk.

I decided to move to the town where two of my sisters lived. We were the only three left in our family. My sisters began to look for an apartment for me and they found one – a nice one – and I moved. There, I had to use a taxi service and that got rather expensive.

I needed to find a church to attend. There was no Assembly of God church in town, and I didn't want to travel out of town. There was a Baptist church in town and I started to go there. But soon after, the taxi service decided not to have Sunday business.

The first Sunday at the Baptist church a certain lady named Brenda came and introduced herself to me. We talked for a couple of minutes. She asked me where I lived and she told me she lived only a few blocks from me. Then she said she had to leave. At that moment I wondered how I would get to church the next Sunday. I called after her and asked her if she could pick me up for church. She readily agreed to do that. For the next two years, she faithfully came by and I got into her car. In those two years, we became good friends.

Well, there came the day when two of her elderly relatives passed away. It was rather close together, date-wise, and Brenda told me about these two dear Christians.

They each had a car, and they desired to give them to Brenda. A couple of weeks passed, and she got word the family was going to bring a car to her. It was a Subaru with only 3,000 miles on it. It was just like new. Brenda told me, "Betty, as soon as they bring the car to me" (she got a little emotional), "I am going to give my car to you." Within a week, she and her son picked me up and took me to get all the necessary arrangements made. Then she handed the key to me and said, "It is yours, Betty. Take it and drive home!"

The Ravens Do It Again
Vivian Dippold

My husband Otto was called into the ministry when he was twelve years old. In all his school years in New Jersey, he would tell whoever asked about his future that he was going to be a preacher. His classmates knew it and so did his neighbors. He preached for over 50 years until he went to be with the Lord in 2018.

However, preaching was only one of the gifts he was given. He was a contractor, builder and organizer. In every church he pastored, there was a building that needed to be built. He did the work needed with the stipulation that the church would not go into debt. Of course, God prepared the congregation and they were willing to make it happen.

One of the building miracles happened when he accepted the pastorate in Lansdale, PA. The congregation had purchased a choice piece of land many years before, but they were reluctant to move on to build a new sanctuary. Ott was full of faith and knew that God would provide if they stepped out in faith. He didn't begin a building program, just asked for those who would give to a building fund. When the money was there, the work would start.

One Sunday morning, an older couple, whom my husband readily recognized as neighbors from his childhood home in New Jersey, came in and sat in the back. Nothing strange about that, except that they were ardent Jehovah's Witnesses.

After the service, the couple greeted Ott with a huge hug and explained that they were now Believers in Jehovah and would be attending our church. They attended faithfully and were aware that funds were needed to start this building project.

After several weeks, the couple pulled my husband aside and asked how much was needed to begin the work. (I can't remember the exact amount, but somewhere around $30,000.) The woman nonchalantly opened her purse and pulled out a HUGE envelope filled with hundred-dollar bills tightly wound in groups with rubber bands. She counted out the amount needed and placed the musty-smelling bundles in Ott's hand. We joked about where they might have been stored. We later discovered the couple didn't trust banks! They were well off, but because there were family members still in the Jehovah's Witnesses, the couple wanted to remain anonymous.

We were curious about how they had come to the church and the woman told us they had just moved to Lansdale. She remembered that Otto had become a minister. After they accepted Christ, they looked up his name to see where he was. As God would have it, he was also in Lansdale, too, pastoring the local Assemblies of God church.

The work on a section of the new building began the next week. Today, the building still stands as a testimony of God's faithfulness. We never know just when, where or by whom God will send His ravens and supply the need.

Memories in a Nutshell
Betty Martin

My husband Asa and I met at a youth rally. I played the piano for the rally and when he saw me, he thought, "That's the girl for me." The next week I received a letter from him asking if he could come to see me. We had our first date in 1940.

We were both brought up in Assembly of God homes. I was very happy. We were married for fifty-two years and we have three children. They all are serving the Lord.

Being over ninety years old, it sometimes feels that I have lived two lifetimes. The Lord has been faithful to me. I live near my son Kenneth and his wife Marlene. I find God's Word is like refreshing rain that brings new life to open hearts and meets us in our needs.

Revival, Children, and a Set of China
Mari Lynn Richter

Revival

One time a Lutheran pastor that we knew very well, said that a church needs a genuine revival every ten years. That statement is so true. In one church we were experiencing a revival. People were getting saved and filled with the Spirit. We had a church packed with youth sitting in the front on the floor. Many times, during revival, there will be some people who are against the influx of new people for one reason or another. People who embrace the move of God will grow spiritually and progress in their spiritual walk. God is still God and desires for us to press hard into His ways.

Children

One time when the kids were almost old enough to be out of the house, they were talking about how they didn't have certain things growing up as there was never enough money. I looked at them and asked, "Did you ever go without shelter?" "No," they replied. "Did you ever not have food to eat?" "No." "Did you ever not have clothes on your back and that wasn't clean?" The answer again was "No." Many times, no matter the age, our children need to know that God did not leave them or forget them.

China

I didn't have any really good dishes. I liked to have people over for meals but felt like I never had enough dishes. I started praying for a nice set of dishes not even for China but just a nice set.

One day the wife of the Assistant Superintendent of the District called and said that she had received two sets of dishes, including a set of China for twelve. She felt that she should give one set to me. I chose the set for twelve. Every time I used those dishes, I am reminded of how God wants to bless us abundantly. Many people have eaten off those dishes and I am blessed each time I use them. Miracles never grow old.

Provision Above and Beyond
Arlene Grabill

I became a Christian at the age of ten.

My husband Paul and I met at the Eastern District Youth Chorale. I sang and Paul played the piano.

Our first church was a home missions work in Chadds Ford, PA. From there we moved to Irwin and then to State College.

I have experienced God's intervention in a very clear way in my life. I had a serious skiing accident. My injuries consisted of six broken bones in my face, a punctured lung, and many facial lacerations from the ice and rocks.

There were financial pressures before the accident, but the doctors' bills were staggering. We were left with a bill of $25,000. This bill was totally forgiven by the doctors, the hospital, and others involved.

Pattern For Prayer
Rev. Elsie Ezzo

Lord, help me to draw a Pattern for Prayer
Help me to intercede for the Lost!
In every day that I live and breathe
That people may find Hope at any cost!

Help me to trust the Lord always,
And lean not on my own wisdom and power!
Help me to be a well-watered garden,
And display God's fruit and beautiful flowers!

Help me to meditate on your Word -
It feeds my Spirit and Soul!
Help me to hear and do Your Will!
To be like Jesus is my Goal!

Memories of Life's Journey
Faye White

I was raised in a Christian home with godly parents who were great examples. My mother led me to the Lord at the altar when I was five years old. It was during a children's crusade with Rev. Charles Shaffer. I received the Baptism in the Holy Spirit when I was nine years old. At a Youth Convention in Hershey, I responded to an altar call for those who would serve God as a pastor, missionary or pastor's wife. A month later I met Gordon! We were introduced by mutual friends. After we were married, we answered the call to pastor at Northeast Assembly of God in Philadelphia, PA.

We had some wonderful experiences there with great friends. Three of our children were born while we were there.

My mother was in poor health, so we moved to Tucson, AZ. There I received both my Bachelor's and Master's degrees at the University of Arizona. Moving to Holbrook, I began teaching math at the high school. About a third of the students were Navajo and Hopi. I also had the privilege of helping at the Indian Mission with missionaries Gene and Marion Herd.

Ever since we were children, Gordon and I both felt a call to missions. So, with some direction from Springfield, we left for French language study and then on to the Ivory Coast. There we faced difficulties with sicknesses, hard travel on bad roads and children at boarding school. God blessed us and we were able to establish several village churches.

Our second term was in Togo, West Africa training young pastors at the Bible school. We certainly learned to trust God for our needs. Gordon could have told you many stories about our experiences there. After our retirement, we served as missionary associates in Paris, France, helping to establish an English-speaking church.

Gordon went to be with his Lord in January 2014. I miss him terribly, but I realized that there were many widows in our church and the area. So, I am directing a Widow's Support group each week at Hamlin Assembly of God. I also volunteer as a math tutor at Wayne County Adult Literacy Program. God is still able to use the gifts He has given me.

My Life
Rev. Betty Sprowls

It seems I have been a Christian my whole life. When I was young, I would sit on my bed and read the Bible to an imaginary group of people. I started teaching Sunday School before I was a teenager. While in high school, I took the youth group to a retreat. It was there, around a bonfire, that I dedicated my life to God.

I have pastored for over twenty-six years, twenty years of which were in the Presbyterian Church as a lay pastor. I have learned that *"I can do all things through Christ Jesus who strengthens me."* Philippians 4:13 (KJV)

All my life I could not get up in front of people and talk. Yet, God gave me the ability, desire and love to preach His Word. It is only through Him that I was able to do it.

I Remember It Well
Beverly Clute

I was eight years old when the Japanese attacked Pearl Harbor. We had just joined my dad who had been working in Alaska. My brother and I had to pack gas masks to go to school, and there were blackouts and practice alerts.

My mother saw to it that we were in church every service. At the age of twelve, I gave my heart to Jesus, in a log church where I had helped peel the logs.

I met my future husband, LaVerne, who was a soldier in the Air Force, during a street meeting my pastor held with the youth every Sunday night. He followed us back to the church that evening and gave his heart to the Lord. We married a year and a half later.

From the time he graduated till going Home, we pastored for forty-one years. I wouldn't trade those years for anything.

Left Assured
Rev. Bryan Koch
I'm All Right, Copyright 2017, Reprinted with permission.

Maybe you feel like you've been left holding the bag because of life's circumstances. But I want to assure you that you can be "all right."

In the first message that I preached after the accident, I shared the story of Moses leading the Israelites out of Egypt. Here they were, the entire nation of Israel, at the foot of the Red Sea with the Egyptian army close behind. Between a rock and a hard place. And what does God do? He parts the sea, and they walk right through.

Fast forward a bit and you'll find those same Israelites wandering around in the hot, dry desert, complaining that God hasn't delivered them into the Promised Land, and forgetting God's past provision. The problem is that they were living in the future instead of seeking God in their present. They couldn't be patient and wait for God's plan to unfold, and like the psalmist says in Psalm 106:13-14, *"But they soon forgot what he had done and did not wait for his plan to unfold. In the desert they gave in to their craving; in the wilderness, they put God to the test."* (NIV)

The Israelites learned the power of forgetting and the problem with sameness. When you're in a difficult season, it's all too easy to focus on your circumstances and what's happening right now. Trust me, I know! 2014 was undoubtedly one of the hardest years I've ever been through. Facing the birth of our first grandson without Lynn, and then going through the holidays without her was painful. And it could have been easy to wonder where God was in all of this.

But there's importance in remembering when you're walking in the deepest of valleys, the things that God has done in your past. And there's hope and joy in seeking out the ways God is working in your present pain. If biblical hope is confident expectation and biblical joy is intentional and eternal, then being hopeful and joyful in hard circumstances is a choice.

We wake up each day and have to make the choice to find hope and joy in the ways God is working in the present because whether we can see it or not, He has already made a way through it.

There's a Swahili proverb that used the phrase "Haba Nah aba," which translates to "little by little" and has become something of a motto for me. In times of blinding pain and grief, in times of great difficulty, when we reach those hard places, God brings us through. We might not see the big picture, and we might not know the path, but little by little He guides us.

If God brings you to it, He'll bring you through it. All we need to do is remember what God did in our past. Look for God in our present, and trust God with our future. I've lost my left eye, my left leg, and the wedding ring off my left finger, but because of God's grace, mercy, and incredible love, I'm All Right.

I am trusting that wherever life's circumstances have left you, you will find hope, strength and joy knowing that God is right beside you with every step you take.

Strong and Surrendered,
Bryan Koch

Salvation, Wedding, Ministry, & Miracles
Muriel Hobson

I cannot pinpoint a date as to when I became God's child. My unsaved parents sent me to a Presbyterian Church that preached the Gospel. Sunday mornings, I absorbed everything that was taught from God's Word. When I began attending church services, I came to realize that I had been saved sometime during the previous years. I can't remember when, but I knew I had.

I met my husband at a Jack Wyrtzen Youth Rally that was held weekly in New York City. We dated for 1½ years and were married in 1948.

Our first church was of a Baptist denomination in Jacksonville, NC. We had not yet been baptized in the Spirit. After we received this gift of the Spirit, we joined the Assembly of God church.

A great miracle in our family happened when our older daughter had an eye problem, requiring her to wear an eye patch. The doctor said having a television would be beneficial to her eyes. We did not have any money to buy one, so a member of the church very generously provided one. Another time while living in New Jersey, I had a bladder problem. I didn't feel I would be able to make a trip to Maine to visit my daughter's family. While taking communion one Sunday morning, the Lord healed me, and I made that 13-hour trip with no problem!

Amazing Grace
Lorraine Swank

My grandmother was saved in the early 1930s. She witnessed to and prayed for her family. Then my parents were saved. I was in an Assembly of God church from age six but never gave my heart to Jesus until I was seventeen.

I was saved at the Freeport Gospel Tabernacle in Freeport, PA, which is now Sarver Evangel Heights A/G. This was 1948 and I was filled with the Holy Spirit and baptized in water that same year. I was a junior in high school and dating Johnnie who wanted no part of my "religion." There were several young people saved that year, and one of them was Jim Swank who became a good friend of my brother. He came to the church and got saved one month after I did.

Jim said that when he saw me in the youth choir, he fell for me and wanted to date me. The church was praying that Johnnie would get saved, and Jim prayed for him also. But he said he added to his prayer, "If Johnnie refuses to be saved, could I please have Lorraine?"

Johnnie and I broke up a couple of months later. Jim, being at our home often, knew when that happened. It wasn't long until he asked me to go to a Singspiration with him, and he would take me for rides in his car. We both fell "head over heels" in love with each other. Jim was totally committed to Christ and the church. I soon realized that if I wanted to be his girl, I had to be also! We were married two years later, and I am forever grateful that God gave me Jim Swank!

Thirty Years of Back Pain, GONE!
Nancy J. Lundmark

My husband Daniel E. Lundmark pastored Northampton Assembly of God, Northampton, PA, for fifty years before his promotion to heaven in 2019. During those years, the Lord proved Himself faithful in many ways as we served Him.

One particular testimony of the healing of a Catholic lady named Mary has come to mind recently. My husband also wrote a weekly column in the newspapers. Years after this incident, he described the healing in one of his columns:

"I well remember the first time Mary attended our church in 1971, with several of her relatives. That Sunday night I became aware of abnormal pain in my back and concluded that the Lord was revealing to me the pain of another. I described the pain and asked if anyone who was having that pain would like to come forward for prayer. Mary later testified that she thought at the time that it couldn't be her, since I had never met her before and did not know that she had gone regularly to the doctor for thirty years for a severe back problem. Then, she felt hands from behind prodding her to go forward. Thinking it was her relatives nudging her to go up for prayer, Mary started up the aisle. Halfway up, she turned around to see who it was.

To her amazement no one was there—it was the hand of the Lord on her, encouraging her to go for prayer in the unfamiliar church surroundings. When we prayed for her, the Lord miraculously and immediately healed her! Mary was amazed—the back pain was gone!

She no longer needed her medications and doctor—she was fully healed! Mary was convinced that Jesus Christ is *"the same yesterday, and today, and forever"* as Hebrews 13:8 states. She found Him to be her Healer and more importantly— her Savior! Mary placed her entire trust in Jesus for her salvation and regularly attended our church service for 30 years until her passing in 2003."

(by the late Rev.Daniel E. Lundmark)

Memories of Mary Jeanne (Sneath) Myers
As told to her family

John J. Myers and Mary Jeanne Sneath met at Benny's Place, a dance hall in Quarryville, PA. They soon began their courtship. Little time passed before John gave Jeanne a music box that contained an engagement ring inside. Shortly afterward they were married. Two years after their wedding John and Jeanne moved to Green Lane, PA, where John entered the Eastern Bible Institute for a three-year course of study.

Throughout the years, John was a part-time pastor and Sunday School Teacher at various Assembly of God churches. He and Jeanne held several jobs to support their family.

Jeanne diligently kept a household going for her seven children and husband. She sewed many dresses throughout the years, cooked meals, and saw to it that their children had music lessons and the chance to participate in various sports.

Laughter was frequent at the Myers' home and it was a healing balm. To the delight of her children, Jeanne humorously "made the animals talk." Jeanne had a special voice that gave pets and wild animals a voice making them a participant in the household. Throughout the years the family had canaries, cars, St. Bernard dogs, mutts, chickens, ponies and horses—and they all talked.

During retirement, John and Jeanne took up golf and they had many fun afternoons on Lancaster County gold courses. John made his first hole-in-one and Jeanne was there to witness it.

These are the Moments We Hold in Our Hands
*Contributed by: daughter, Pamela,
as told by Barbara Recene*

On January 7, 2014, my husband of fifty-seven years stepped into Eternity without me. We had a beautiful memorial service in the church. There was not enough room in the church. My son Jim and his wife Anna sang the song my husband would ask me to sing for him, "These Are the Moments We Hold In Our Hands." Kind people of the church made dinner for me and my family. We filled the church, the bottom of the church and the parsonage.

After everyone left, I went to bed, feeling all alone. Over the next few months, I found myself overcome by grief. I could literally feel grief well up within me so deeply it would awaken me. The grief was so bad I would often walk the floors and wail. These were the days when I found that Jesus bore my grief and sorrows. I also realized that some of this grief was not of God, but God did allow my tears for a reason. He holds those tears in a bottle because they are precious to Him. Soon, the grief began to ease up.

A while before my husband's passing, Gracie, the cat, showed up at the house. My husband had said to not let the cat in because she would cause too much stress. She never tried to enter the house until he died. One day, I opened the door and in came Gracie who became my companion for the next few years.

God's Continued Comfort and Provision
Barbara Recene

After the passing of my husband, I found that going to church helped me a lot. One Sunday as I walked in, I felt God say, "The rest of your life will be the best of your life." And it has been. The church invited me to remain in the parsonage for the rest of my life. Over the years they have cared for me and my children. The church gathered around me doing their best to meet any and every need we had. They even had a new gas furnace installed in the parsonage. I have been privileged to live here for years now and I am very appreciative.

My youngest daughter SueEllen came to live with me after she was diagnosed with a rare and aggressive form of melanoma. Over the next several months we traveled every other day to Geisinger Hospital in Danville, PA. My daughter Pamela left her home in Kauai and moved in to help me with SueEllen. For ten days straight we traveled back and forth to Geisinger. SueEllen was suffering greatly and lived one day after being placed in hospice.

The joy of the Lord came into us the day SueEllen passed. We rejoiced because we knew she had entered eternity with her Lord and the suffering was over. That Sunday morning our pastor held a beautiful service. It was perfect.

The presence of God coming down has been the greatest comfort in my life. We have climbed many mountains since the passing of my husband John James. After SueEllen's passing, for the first time, I felt that I killed the lion, the bear, and I could do this. I can make it because Jesus is right here with me. I am not alone.

My Salvation
Rev. Connie Homerski

My mother was my greatest inspiration as far as serving the Lord is concerned. She prayed often and sang hymns daily. We were in church every Sunday. It was at church that I learned about salvation through Jesus Christ. During one of these services, I heard the Lord speak to my heart. I went up to the altar and accepted Jesus Christ as my personal Lord and Savior.

At the age of sixteen, I was working in a local restaurant. Shortly after starting my job, I was approached by another waitress who coaxed me into trying a cigarette. I had never smoked a day in my life. All it took was one cigarette and I was hooked. Over the next sixteen years, this habit got out of control and I was up to smoking two packs a day.

It was when my four-year-old started crying and said, "Mommy, why don't you quit smoking?" I began to cry, too. I tried many times, but I couldn't quit. One Sunday night, I went to an Assembly of God church, knelt at the altar, and with all my heart cried: "God deliver me or kill me!" I walked out of the church completely delivered! Praise the Lord!

One night after a Sunday evening service, I came home, opened my Bible and laid it on a chair. I looked down and saw these words, *"Study to show thyself approved unto God a workman that needeth not to be ashamed, rightly dividing the Word of Truth."* 2 Timothy 2:15 (KJV) I then heard God speak to me and say, "You're going into the ministry."

After joining the Assembly of God church, I received the baptism of the Holy Spirit with the evidence of speaking in tongues. It has been my greatest joy. It has also been my greatest joy to serve the Lord through the years. Preaching, teaching and singing His praises. I have seen people saved, healed and serving the Lord. Now I am waiting to meet the Master face to face.

Testimony of My Salvation
Rev. Lawane Hahn

I was not born into a Christian home, but when I was ten years old a friend and I went to the Episcopal church. There I served as an altar boy and was confirmed. The pastor was a wonderful man, but he never taught me about salvation.

Years passed, and shortly after my wife and I were married, we visited friends in Wilkes Barre, PA. It was there that I saw an advertisement on TV for an Oral Roberts healing service in Pittston, PA. I didn't know what it was all about, but something drew me.

We went to the first service and as we walked under the tent, we felt something going through our bodies. We didn't know at the time that this was the power of the Holy Spirit. That evening my Uncle Charles, my mother-in-law, my parents and sisters attended the service with us. We saw many miracles and were drawn to the altar to be saved. We didn't know what this was all about, but we wanted it. On the way home from the service, my sister began screaming and saying her poison ivy was completely gone. Later that night when my mother went to the bathroom, she noticed her ankles were not puffed up like they normally were. They were both completely healed and never stood in a prayer line.

We saw countless miracles in these services, but I will only highlight only a few. Clubfeet were healed and a seven-year-old's eyes were opened. A fourteen-year-old boy jumped out of his wheelchair and ran the length of the tent.

I will never forget the young woman, who was healed from blindness, running around the tent screaming, "I am going home to see my baby for the first time!" People were brought on stretchers and some were completely healed from cancer. Demons were cast out of people. I remember the police officers kneeling in the tent with tears running down their faces. One night there was a bad thunderstorm and we walked through it to get to the tent. When we got inside, my wife and I both noticed we were completely dry and our shoes were clean. Now that is the power of God. We attended all ten services and were never the same again. We began growing in the Lord and looking for a church to attend that was not dead, like the one where we were going.

We attended The Wesleyan church for about ten years and really grew in the Lord. I even served as the assistant pastor for a time. God used me in altar ministry and souls were saved and lives were touched. We didn't realize at that time that there were more things of the Spirit we had not yet experienced. We were invited to another church; the night we attended, my wife and I received the baptism of the Holy Spirit. We were so excited about this that we shared it with our current pastor. He did not believe in the gifts of the Holy Spirit and we were asked to move on from the church. We began attending Northampton Assembly of God. We grew more in the Lord and began to experience more of the things of the Spirit.

God's Faithfulness and Provision
Rev. Loretta M. Jacobs

It all started many years ago when a church that my husband and I pastored set aside monies in an account for retirement. This was part of the benefits package. My husband had "opted" out of Social Security years before pastoring this church. Each church that we pastored thereafter agreed to keep this benefit going. Once my husband and I retired, this retirement account was helpful as a part of our income. This has been such a blessing through the years. God prepared us for retirement, despite our poor choice with Social Security and I am so grateful!

Some years ago, after my husband went home to be with Jesus, my daughter and I were coming home from church the Sunday before Thanksgiving. We were traveling on a back road through the woods. There was a deer, a big doe, that came running alongside the car and then ran into the driver's side front fender putting a hole in the fender. My daughter handled the driving very well through this incident. The doe ended up on her back in the middle of the road. Then she got up and ran into the woods. At the time, my car was older and I did not have it fully insured.

I didn't know where the money would come from to pay for the repairs. My daughter and I put the money down that was required to purchase the parts. This was only half of the money needed for the repairs. The rest of the repair money God provided through two unexpected sources. We had the money when it was needed to pay the rest of the repair bill.

God was Faithful and sent in the means for our need!

Recently, I was having an electrical situation in the house where the lights were "flickering" and "dimming/powering down" for several days. After having some family members here for the day, it seemed like the furnace should be checking in, but didn't. My daughter checked the thermostat and the furnace was not checking in when the temperature was raised. She called the furnace man. He came and discovered that the "brains" of our furnace were fried. The furnace man was able to repair and replace the fried part that night. The part and service calls were not an expense I was expecting at Christmas time. He suggested to my daughter that she call the electric company to have the electricity checked. The electric company came out and assessed the outside wires. The main wire from the house to the transformer had been repaired several times. The technician replaced the older wire, free of charge. The electrical "flickering" and "dimming/powering down" had stopped. I was able to pay the bill when the furnace man was here. Within the next few days, God provided the furnace repair money from unexpected sources.

God is so good and meets our every need! I praise Him for His faithfulness and provision! God is always on time and protects His own. If you give your tithes and offerings to the Lord, you will not lack for any need you have, as He is Faithful! Two of my favorite scriptures are:

"Trust in the LORD with all thine heart; and lean not unto thine own understanding."
       - Proverbs 3:5-6 and Matthew 6:33 (KJV)

The Writing on the Wall
Rev. Lorna Albanese

September 26, 2021, is a significant day in my grief journey. It marks the first time I went to a Steelers game since my husband Danny died. I had been thinking about this day for a long time wondering what it might be like. What would Seat 18 in Row B of Section 536 be like without him there? It's hard to imagine him not at the stadium Sundays at 1:00—after all, he'd been a regular at games for more than forty years.

He started going to Steelers games with his uncle a year before Chuck Knoll was hired. They got season tickets and football became one of "their things." They shared many epic football moments together. They saw the Immaculate Reception in person and went to three out of the four winning Super Bowls in the '70s. For some reason they decided not to go to the first one in Pittsburg. A bad decision and they said "never again" after that. They enjoyed football together for decades. Once his uncle was unable to go to the games any longer because of health reasons, Steelers games with Danny became one of "our things."

Home games became a part of the rhythm of our fall and winter Sundays. We'd eat a bag lunch in the car after church on the way to the game and stop for a sandwich at Primanti's on the way home from the stadium. We'd be entertained by the tailgaters during the walk from our parking spot to the stadium. We'd kiss when the Steelers scored a touchdown and heckled when they stunk. We even got to attend the winning Super Bowl XL together in Detroit.

Today, when I entered Gate A, right in front of me I see a wall of names. I've walked by it many times before and never paid attention to it. This time, it grabbed my attention and I decided to look more closely at it. It was the names of the season ticket holders when Heinz Field was built. I found his name in less than a minute. Seeing it put a smile on my face and a tear in my eye. As scores of people entered the stadium and walked by, I stood there and reflected on the many games we shared together at Heinz Field, kissed his name (via my fingers), and then went to "our" seats.

Grief journeys are about finding a new normal in each aspect of life. Today I discovered a new normal for game days at Heinz Field. Whenever I go to a game, my experience is going to include a moment of reflection and appreciation at that wall. I won't run out of football memories any time soon, so I can keep going to a lot more games.

The Simple Small Spot
Dorcas Chavez

One of the physical signs of getting older is getting more age spots than you'd like. Sometimes grandchildren even make a connect-the-dot game out of them! One day, one of those dots didn't look good to my son and that turned into a trip to the doctor. The diagnosis was melanoma, a more aggressive skin cancer.

My husband and I had already planned a two-month mission trip to Chile, South America. I thought I would have a biopsy done when I returned from the trip. I trusted God for my healing and knew that He was in control.

After a successful and fruitful trip, I followed through with the procedure and waited for the final confirmation, which proved to be what the doctor said. It was this procedure that led to a larger piece being removed to make sure the cancer was not spreading. All the time I was trusting and praying for my complete healing.

Well, after 1 ½ years and after many follow-up visits, I can say I'm cancer-free. I praise the Lord for it!

Psalm 91:14 (NIV) *"Because he loves me, says the Lord, I will rescue him. I will protect him for he acknowledges My name."*

Memories from my Past
Carolyn Leeper

I didn't become a Christian until I was an adult. We already had two girls, and I was pregnant with our third child. The doctor said there were many complications and suggested that I have an abortion. A healthy baby girl was born in December. It was then we realized that God had been responsible for her healing, and we both accepted Christ. Another healing was when I was working and injured my neck. I had a lot of pain, but after a while, God poured His healing on me, and since then I have been pain-free.

I first met Lewis after my parents rented the farm across the street from his family. I was sixteen and he was nineteen. We dated for a year and then got married. When Lewis decided he needed to go to Bible school, we headed to Northeast Bible Institute (currently University of Valley Forge). At that time, we had five children. It was a hard time financially. One day, we didn't have any food in the house and the only money we had was the tithe from Lewis's paycheck. We decided to trust the Lord and give the tithe and God proved Himself true. We never had a problem with not having food in the house the rest of the school terms. After Lewis graduated from Northeast Bible Institute, we accepted a small home missions church in West Virginia. It was a wonderful experience.

My Remembrance
Written by daughter as remembered by: Dottie Lewis

I was newly married when my husband Cliff Lewis took me to Padre Island, off the coast of Texas, where he had been establishing a church in Port Aransas. In 1948, it was not a resort island. It was sparsely populated and inhabited mostly by fishermen.

Cliff and I worked alongside the members of the church, (only twenty-five to thirty people at the time) to build the structure of the little church. The Presbyterian church down the road also gave us a hand. We rented a small little cottage from a widow who was a church member and lived next door.

There was no salary, but we were paid from the Sunday morning offering, which at times could be as little as four dollars. We never went hungry. People would leave food at our door and invite us over for dinner. Fishermen would leave "the catch of the day" in our sink. I learned to appreciate fresh fish.

I had my first child over on the mainland at a small hospital in Aransas Pass. My daughter asked me how we afforded to pay for the hospital (it was pre-insurance) and I said, "I don't know, I can't remember". I do know I was treated royally. My son and I were the only ones in the maternity ward at the time. We learned to really trust in the Lord, in that little start-up work, as day after day God provided for us in all ways!

I am reminded of the passage in Matthew chapter six that Jesus teaches on "worry." In essence, verses 25-34 says:

"Therefore I tell you, do not worry about your life, what you will eat or drink or about your body, what you will wear. Is not life more important than food, and the body more important than clothes? Look at the birds of the air, they do not sow or reap or store away in barns, and yet your heavenly Father feeds them. Are you not much more valuable than they? Who of you by worrying can add a single hour to his life?

And why do you worry about clothes? See how the lilies of the field grow. They do not labor and spin...will he not much more clothe you, O you of little faith...But seek first his kingdom and his righteousness, and all these things will be given to you as well. Therefore, do not worry about tomorrow, for tomorrow will worry about itself. Each day has enough trouble of its own." (NIV)

A Time to Laugh
Rev. Florence Bogdan

My husband Stephen and I grew up attending Highway Tabernacle and it was there we also were married. In 1979, we returned to Highway where we pastored until 1999.

When I was pregnant with our daughter Bonnie, I had eclampsia. It had gotten so severe that I was rushed to the hospital by an ambulance, which also served as the funeral home hearse. I laugh today and say, "I rode in a hearse and lived to tell about it."

Romans 8:28 says, *"We know that all things work together for good to them that love God, to them who are the called according to his purpose."* (KJV)

Note: Florence has since passed to her Heavenly reward, but she left behind some choice chuckle moments.

Quotes from Florence:
- "As the years roll by, we might as well laugh!"
- "A friend once told me I was born before the Dead Sea knew it was sick."
- "One doctor said, 'Cheerful people live longer…the early birds get the germs.'"
- "I was the only person that could say they rode in the back of a hearse and lived to tell about it." (In those days, the hearse doubled for an ambulance!)
- "At eighty-six, I really am "good for nothing." That scoundrel "Arthur-Ritis" has wrecked my knees leaving me without a good leg on which to stand. My nephew says I am now a "Cane-a-nite."

Everything Changes
Rev. Sharon Poole

The death of a spouse or partner is different than other losses, in the sense that it literally changes every single thing in your world going forward. When your spouse dies, the way you eat changes. The way you watch TV changes. Your friend circle changes (or disappears entirely). Your family dynamic/life changes (or disappears entirely). Your financial status changes. Your job situation changes. It affects your self-worth. Your self-esteem. Your confidence. Your rhythms. The way you breathe. Your mentality. Your brain function. (Ever heard the term 'widow brain?' If you don't know what that is, count yourself as very lucky.) Your physical body, your hobbies, and your interests. Your sense of security. Your sense of humor. Your sense of womanhood or manhood. EVERY SINGLE THING CHANGES. You are handed a new life that you never asked for and that you don't particularly want. It is the hardest, most gut-wrenching, horrific, life-altering of things to live it.

Wedding Vows
Rev. Lorna Albanese

Thirty years ago, when I stood at the altar and said "in sickness and in health" I didn't realize the depths of those words. Thinking of Danny today.

Good Words of Advice
Roberta Anderson

Stay close to the Lord.
Immerse yourself in the Word of God.
Find an older, more mature, pastor's wife who you feel
comfortable confiding in.
Find a pastor's wife who can mentor you
as you share with her.
And don't try to please everyone, just please God.

Words of Wisdom
Rev. Ralph Volpe

**Keep your SON glasses on,
because your future in Christ Jesus
keeps getting brighter and brighter**

My Advice for Young Couples Just Starting in Ministry!
Celeste Falvo

After both receiving the call to full-time ministry on the same night, at the same exact time, my husband Dave and I knew we had heard from God. Dave had just been promoted at his job and he was making more money than we could have ever imagined! Now we had a call on our lives, and we were obedient and started the process.

My husband went on to become an assistant pastor and I taught in their pre-school. We were thrilled to be operating in our calling, but we lacked experience. We really needed guidance in those early days. There were so many adjustments and mistakes. I noticed myself trying to be someone else. I'm quiet by nature, more of a wallflower, but I tried to be outgoing. I was struggling. Meanwhile, Dave was a "people-person" and wasn't struggling with the transition as much.

I realized what I needed was a mentor. This is my biggest encouragement to young couples in full-time ministry. Find a mentor. I was blessed with two of them! Dave and I also had a mentor for us as a couple. I'd suggest finding two sets of mentors: one outside the ministry and one mature in ministry. Now, as a widow, I still use what I was taught by my mentors to help encourage those who are grieving or need a listening ear.

Here are three important things that I learned from my mentors that I would like to pass on:

1. God, His Word and your communication with Him is the most important thing. If this relationship is good, everything else will fall into place.

2. Always be true to yourself. You may look up to someone and glean from their lives, but you are not them. You are uniquely designed by God. You have strengths and faults, and that's okay. You will be amazed at how much better you can minister when you are not worrying about trying to fit a mold or be like someone else.

3. Your family is the most important ministry! After your relationship with God, put your family first. Your marriage/family life is the most vulnerable and it is where the enemy likes to attack. Protect them! Pray constantly for them.

When Dave would officiate weddings, he would give couples three pieces of advice: Remember to say, "Yes, Dear!", "I'll try harder, Dear!" and "I'm Sorry, Dear!" If you are not too stubborn to say those words to your spouse, you will not be too stubborn to do what God is calling you to do.

My one final piece of advice is to always talk to each other! You are a team. Love God and serve Him together with your whole heart, mind and soul. Build your marriage together, raise your family together and THEN your ministry.

There may be tough times, but with God and each other, you will survive!

For A Younger Pastor's Wife
Lorraine Swank

I am sure that I do not know what it is like to be today's pastor's wife. I was one from 1953 to 1992. Because of my age and ability to look back, I would encourage younger pastor's wives with these words:
- Create all of the warm, fun memories that you can.
- Pray earnestly for your children every day. Family altar times are precious.
- Love your congregation and strive to see them with the eyes of Jesus.
- *"Work hard and cheerfully at whatever you do, as though you were working for the Lord rather than for people."* - Colossians 3:23 (NLT)
- Learn to laugh at yourself.

Advice to Wives in Ministry
Arline Grabill

- Love unconditionally your God, your husband, your children and the congregation God has placed you in …no matter how they respond to you.

- Neither our husbands, children nor ministries will ever be enough for us. Only the One who created our hearts will be able to mend our hearts.

- Our children's shoulders are not big enough to handle our struggles in life. Take your struggles to the Lord or another trusted sister in Christ.

- When, *not if,* you struggle with someone in the congregation, do not vent when your children are around. They will learn to resent those that make you and their dad sad.

- Don't expect the congregation to respect your husband if you don't.

****

There was one time when I was ready to share my frustration with a staff member, whom I believed was being unfair to my son. I told Paul I was going to speak with him. His response to me was: "Are you willing to live with the consequences of telling that person how unfair they are?"

After many tears, the answer was: "No." Not only would I have caused the staff member pain, but I would have lost the respect of my son. Paul said, "The Lord will honor my son; I don't have to."

Sometimes Words Are Not Needed
Rev. Rebecca Richendrfer

Be yourself, be kind, loving, thoughtful and, most of all, be a good listener.

I remember one time when I was about fifty years old, a lady stopped by our home. She began telling me about her many problems. I didn't know what to tell her so mostly I just listened. Later she told me how I was such a help to her that day. All I did was give her a listening ear.

"Carry each other's burdens, in this way you will fulfill the law of Christ." Galatians 6:2 (NIV)

My God Who Strengthens Me
Rev. Janet Giles

In 1975, after a long search, I finally gave my life to Christ in my living room while watching the 700 Club. Then I began to hear about the Baptism in the Holy Spirit. We were always told "tongues" were not from God. But the Lord is so faithful, and He sent a couple and another woman into our group who had already received this Baptism. They shared their experiences and showed us several Scriptures that confirmed it was a separate experience from salvation. I finally reached the point where I knew this was a gift from God and I wanted to experience this gift. One day kneeling by my bed, I asked God for this gift, and I was baptized in the Spirit and began to speak in other tongues. As we seek, God is always faithful to answer.

I met my spouse for the first time when I was in tenth grade at my cousin's graduation party. He and his family were friends of my aunt and uncle's family. I thought he was really cute, but I told my girlfriends that he did not even know I was there. I did not see him again until many years later. He had been home from the Navy for a short time, and I had graduated from business school and was working. We began dating and, in a few months, we made plans to be married. We had been married almost forty years when he passed away.

We served in ministry in Maryland. My husband pastored the church and I was the administrator of our Christian School. The first church I ministered in as a pastor was Hope Assembly of God. I became the pastor in 2012 and was very blessed to have a very supportive loving congregation.

The most amazing time that God provided for our financial needs was when we started our school, Tree of Life. After a couple of years, by God's direction, we moved into a commercial building where we rented four suites. My husband and I gave the rental agent a list of extra things that the school needed to have done. We were told that the extra items could not be done and were not covered in the agreement.

This was a new building still being finished on the inside, so my husband told the agent to just present it to the boss. She did, and when she came back she said, "I don't understand it, but he is going to do it for nothing. I guess the boss you work for is much greater than mine." Praise the Lord. What a witness that was!

Yes, I have experienced great losses in my life: A son was stillborn and my two daughters and husband were taken by PPH (Primary Pulmonary Hypertension) within two years. Through it all, I have found Philippians 4:13 has proven true.

"I CAN do all things through Christ which strengthens me." (KJV)

It All Happened So Fast
Rev. Loretta Jacobs

Shortly after graduating from high school, I married my husband Paul who was already pastoring a church. Things changed rapidly as overnight I became a wife and a pastor's wife at the same time. The challenges we faced led me to what became my favorite scripture in God's Word.

"But seek ye first the kingdom of God and his righteousness, and all these things shall be added unto you." Matthew 6:33 (KJV)

Throughout these years God has proven Himself to me over and over again. I thank God for a husband who taught me how to stand on the Solid Rock, Christ Jesus.

Don't Forget Your Calling!
Barbara Stigile

The LORD called Samuel, and he answered, "Here I am!" I Samuel 3:4

Remember, God, called you with your specific gifts and abilities. He didn't call you to be like the preacher in the next county or a well-known evangelist. When God called you, He had you on His mind!

I still remember when my husband, recently out of Eastern Bible Institute (EBI), was asked to speak at a fellowship meeting. Afterward, an elderly minister from a neighboring town told my husband he should have been a Presbyterian preacher. Back then, in our circles, it was thought you had to be loud and slam the pulpit to be good. I've often thought about that pastor's statement and how different our lives would have been if we had gone to the Presbyterian denomination. Different – yes; in God's will – no.

My husband wanted to be a farmer and had a job working on a farm after his high school graduation. One Sunday that summer, while praying in church, God clearly spoke to Eddie and told him he was to enter the ministry. Eddie told the Lord, "I will if you can have me in Bible school this fall." He thought there was no way that would be possible. He didn't have the money and his parents didn't have the money.

Eddie did enter EBI that fall with his tuition paid. We believe it was paid by one or more Assembly of God churches we both attended, but we never knew for sure. I also think he sold "Ole Bessy," his cow, to contribute. Each year he attended Bible school with expenses paid through faithful donations; when he graduated, there were funds left over that he left for a student in need. You see, Eddie had to be true to God, the sacrificial givers from his home church, and himself. I came to realize he wasn't meant to be a Bible slamming preacher. He taught like Jesus.

Oh, and by the way, God fulfilled Eddie's dream of being a farmer. He plowed the ground and sowed the seed in lives, and God gave the increase. Remember, you aren't responsible for saving souls God is. You are just to be faithful in spreading the seed and watering your plantings with prayer and love.

Taking Things Too Seriously
Rev. Marjorie Richendrfer

In the early days of ministry, while pastoring, I took some things too seriously and soon found my heart filled with lots of painful hurts. It took several years to heal and to regain my self-image and confidence in people. I almost lost confidence in God.

So, praise the Lord! Go to Him in prayer. Stay in His Word, daily. Don't take what people say and do too seriously.

I was once told: "A woman has the power to make or break her husband." I never forgot that and tried to "make" not "break" my loving husband.

When the Wandering Lamb Is Your Own
Dorcas Chavez

Raising three sons was a challenge. Having one of them walk away from God was a nightmare. Our heart's desire was to raise and teach our son in the fear and admonition of the Lord, as it is for every believer, but even more so for a pastor and his wife.

Our son started showing signs of disinterest in church life at the age of sixteen. For whatever reason, it became apparent through the many bad decisions he made that there was no moral conviction when he was confronted with choices. What I thought to be a phase turned out to be a twenty-two-year-long journey that required a lot of prayers and unconditional love.

The one choice we made as husband and wife was not to compromise God's Word and to be consistent in living our faith and model it before our three sons. God's hand of protection, as well as his sovereignty, was evident through the years. This encouraged us to stay before His throne, to intercede and stand in the gap for our son.

Our son's love of family one day opened a door for his sister-in-law and brother to speak to him. Through their witness God's providence and the prayers of those who loved him, helped to soften his heart to respond to his Savior's call. Today, our son's desire is no longer to live for himself, but for Christ. Praise the Lord!

Jesus replied, "Truly I tell you if you have faith and do not doubt, not only can you do what was done to the fig tree, but also you can say to this mountain, 'Go throw yourself into the sea,' and it will be done. If you believe, you will receive whatever you ask for in prayer." Matthew 21:21-22 (NIV)

Prayer: Lord, I will intercede for my loved ones and love them unconditionally, regardless of how long it takes for them to turn to You.

Allowing Kids, the Opportunity to Talk
Darlene Fulton

My precious Isabella asked me, "Mommy, is it ok to say, 'I don't like you because you wouldn't let me do what I wanted to do yesterday?' Because I still love you, 'cause you're my very bestest mommy ever."
I gave her a big hug and said, "Yes."

I want her to always feel she can talk to me no matter what.

Just do your best and continue to ask God for help, strength, wisdom, and guidance…and PRAY, PRAY, PRAY.

Sharing the Call
Rev. Maryann Vespa

Today, as I handled my late husband's devotional book that we would read together every evening until he was too weak due to cancer, tears came to my eyes as I remembered the sacredness of Dave's divine "call" to the ministry.

Even though I too have a "call," I had the privilege to share in his "call." Jesus, himself, had a supernatural way of blending our two "calls" together as we both ministered for many years here in the United States as well as in Ghana, West Africa.

The pictures I hold dearest of Dave are when he is on the platform clutching his Bible, message notes in hand, ready and anxious to preach with all his heart. The expression in his eyes, when he stood behind the pulpit, would reveal that "call" he had in his heart. I sensed, his mission deeply because God willed that I share in that "call."

Ministering Side By Side
Rev. Betty Swank

In 1960 my husband John and I were appointed home missionaries and began our ministry working with the Yaqui Indians. We pioneered an Indian church in Tucson, AZ. In 1968 John was named the state director for Teen Challenge of Arizona. In 1973 we were appointed as foreign missionaries to Mexico where we established an indigenous Teen Challenge work. Fourteen years later we returned to the USA as national home missionaries working with Teen Challenge in Arizona.

Remembering God's Ways in Our Ministry
Maxine Lockett

I was saved when I was 10 years old. Years later, I met my husband at the Living Waters Church Camp in Cherry Tree, PA. Our first church was in Carbondale, PA. It was a small church, but we had such wonderful people. We learned from them as we ministered to them.

God always provides. One memory was when my husband had heart surgery. I asked Brother Clifford Lewis to fill in one Sunday morning at Wrightsville. After the service, I gave him an envelope with a check made out to him. To my surprise that next week, I received a letter from him with the check and a note that read: "You need this more than I do." I will never forget his kindness.

God has healed me many times, but one time specifically, I was suffering from back problems that twisted my back in the shape of a question mark. I was in terrible pain. God healed me and I straightened up as I was supposed to.

A funny memory was when my husband and I were attending District Council. We were eating our lunch at a large table with other ministers when one minister stood up and said loudly, "I have a question." Everyone went silent. "Why are most preacher's kids so bad?" Another minister stood up and replied, "Because they play with the deacon's kids!" We all broke into laughter.

Serving with All My Heart
Rev. Elsie Ezzo

I was born in China to missionary parents. We lived there through my elementary years until the communist government forced my family to leave the country.

Before marrying my husband Domenick, I was already a licensed minister with the Assemblies of God. In 1953, I was ordained. Domenick and I pastored four churches in the New York and New Jersey districts. We also ministered through kids' crusades and camps. I spoke at women's retreats, taught Bible studies, and served as a children's evangelist.

Note: *On March 16, 2013, Elsie was honored for sixty years of ministry.*

Six Years Later
Karen Loose

February 6, 2022, marked the sixth anniversary of Dennis' passing on to heaven and into the presence of the Lord. Nothing prepares you for the sudden loss of your spouse of thirty-five years or the loss of a ministry you invested your heart and soul into for over twelve years. Those people, who I thought would be there for me, were not. It was the hardest year of my life, but God saw me through it and provided friends to help ease my sorrow and tremendous pain. I have grown in many ways since that difficult day, especially spiritually. God uses these tough times to reshape us into the people He designed us to be, if we allow Him.

May you find strength in knowing that although my journey has been very difficult, God has provided in amazing ways, so my story gives Him glory. He will do the same thing for you. God never promised to take away all the trials-only that He would be sufficient for each one. He is more than enough and I praise His name!

Reflecting Back
Rev. Sharon Poole

When Paul and I got married fourth-one years ago, we were told that we needed to commit to each other that "two would become one." At first, it was a bit difficult truly becoming one. After a while, it was our natural state of being. That is why now it is so hard to move forward. I must now learn how to be a whole "one" on my own. I am learning it can only be done successfully through the power of Jesus.

Living in and through grief has caused me to understand that I will always carry a sadness with me. I can laugh, have joy, and continue to live, but the sadness will always be there. It is a reminder of a life of love that is gone.

As I navigate a new year, I fight the desire to stay in the old year. It is as if I am leaving more of my husband Paul behind. But I am determined to look for new traditions to begin.

As I reflect on the statements I have made since the passing of Paul. I immediately go back to where I was emotionally when each was written. As odd as this sounds, I continue to "feel" each one. Although I am able to navigate life better, it does seem complicated as each of these thoughts and emotions builds upon the other.

Today, I pray that you will find fulfillment in your tasks, joy within your heart, and strength within your body.

Blessings, my Friend!

Another Year Gone By
Nilli Oliver

Here we are today marking eight years since your promotion and relocation. At times it feels like you've been gone longer, but mostly it feels like yesterday that we had to say hasta luego. I have to tell you that this mourning journey stinks. One minute you're feeling like you can start breathing again then, BAM out of nowhere, a song, a scent, memory hits you and you're doubled over in grief. Our Girls, Dennis, and the Grands are well and missing you every day.

Tonight, to honor you, we do our annual ritual of going out to eat together, to reminisce and to be grateful for the legacy of love you left behind. I sat at the table and look at our treasures and feel profound gratitude that in each of them there is some of you. Truly, the Lord has blest us.

As for me, you'll be amused to know that my hair color now matches yours. Every time I pass a mirror, I get startled by that old silver-haired fox looking back. I know you were a part of the welcoming party when Jo arrived there in January. Tell her and the rest of the family that we love and miss them. As for you, todavia te amo con todo mi corazon.

The Struggle is Real. But God is Greater.
Muriel Hobson

During our first small church pastorate, a very strong, opinionated and outspoken board member said I had told a lie about him. Not then, nor since, have I ever said anything derogatory about a church member or attendee. I spoke to the man about involving me in gossip. He did not tell me what I supposedly had said. I apologized for anything he thought I said about him. He acknowledged my apology. The board member and his wife were somewhat cold toward me, and we resigned from the church a few years later. I do not believe the church members knew about this trying time or they simply ignored it. The key is to forgive wrongdoing and commit the problem to the Lord and find His peace. Accept the person as he is. Jesus has done this for us.

Then there was the time when my husband was in charge of home Bible studies at a large church. He made up lessons for the person teaching each group. One day, he went to his church office only to find his personal items packed in a box. Needing to cut back on church finances, the senior pastor decided to cut back the staff without telling my husband. No one had informed my husband. He came home to pray about the situation and decided to have a meeting with the pastor. The pastor apologized sincerely for having treated us so shabbily. Our salary and health insurance were cut off. We had financial needs. At least the church paid for our health insurance for a few months and did a few other small things for us. We felt uncomfortable worshipping there and left the church a while later.

The key is forgiveness. It isn't always easy to do so immediately. Going through a stressful time for a while may be natural. Since the Lord has forgiven us and continues to do so, we know this is the thing the Lord is waiting for us to do. We did so and peace flooded our hearts. Our faith in trusting HIM for direction concerning our future plans worked out, as it always did before.

Be Ready to Go!
Drucy McDonald

My husband Art used to do things at a moment's notice. He asked me to marry him the week before Christmas. We got our license and blood test and asked the minister to marry us. I got my dress and flowers and asked my cousin to take pictures and make a cake. We announced it to the church and Art and I were married on Tuesday, Christmas Eve, 1985, at 6:30 p.m.

We left for Heritage USA (PTL) on our honeymoon, but we got into a bad snowstorm on Christmas Day. Since it was a holiday, there were limited gas stations open and no food chains open either. We had a good time despite the weather. Many other trips and parties were done in the same spontaneous manner.

His motto was, "Be ready to go at any time!" Oh, I miss him so much!

Make it a Good Day
Doris Sheridan

My husband, Clayton. always said,

> **"Instead of just saying,
> *'I'll try to have a good day,'*
> MAKE it a good day!"**

Being Prepared for Africa?
Rev. Grace Hardt

After graduating from CBC (Central Bible College), my husband David and I were married. Our first church was in Smoke Run, PA. We moved seven times in the first seven years of our marriage.

There were lots of struggles, tears and mistakes, but I learned so much from them. I have no regrets for the life we lived. I didn't mind the hard work. I thought God was preparing me to go to Africa. I have learned if I acknowledge Him, He will direct my path. He keeps me in perfect peace, as long as my mind stays on Him.

Note: Grace attended Calvary Assembly of God in North Huntingdon, the church she and her husband founded in 1972. Grace spent her time visiting shut-ins and going to the nursing home until her passing.

The Three B's
Rev. Ted Graboski

If I were to sit down with a young minister and their spouse, I think I would offer these three "B's" of advice:

Be Humble
When I was a "young" seminarian (I was forty when I answered God's call), I had the privilege of attending a worship time at the seminary chapel. On the platform was an oak pulpit. After the service, I had the chance to go up and stand behind the pulpit and look out into the chapel. A gold plaque was attached to the pulpit's frame facing me. It read, *"Sirs, we would see Jesus."* John 12:21 (KJV).

At that moment, I sensed an awesome feeling of dread in my heart. I admitted, "Who am I that I should even stand, much less speak from this place?" I felt so unworthy, as if all my pride was exposed. I realized then, that whenever I would teach and whatever I would say, I must share Jesus. It must never be about me, but only about Jesus!

I encourage each minister to be humble in his marital relationship. Honor his wife and cherish her. She is your lover, helpmate, friend, support, prayer partner and counselor. Your priorities are first, to God; second, to your spouse and your children; and third, to your calling.

My wife Kathy was my best friend and a great critic of my preaching. When she heard me preach for the first time, she was falling asleep halfway through my message. Afterward, she laughingly kidded me and said, "Honey, never preach your message! Try teaching your message, that is your gift – you are a teacher. I have heard you teach and you are blessed with that ability that God gave you. Use it."

Be Prayerfully Aware
In our first church, I immediately became aware that no matter what else I did as a husband, father and pastor/teacher, prayer was to be my first and constant priority. It was during this first time of ministry that I encountered demonic and occult spiritual presences. My training before ministry was in the natural sciences. I was for all intents and purposes an agnostic with regard to God and spiritual things.
It wasn't until I heard the gospel from a friend of mine that I believed and received Jesus as my Lord and Savior. This church was my introduction to the spiritual dimension and spiritual warfare.

My children and my wife were actually the first to witness angelic visitors in our parsonage. My wife was accustomed to experiencing angelic visitors in her life from the time she was a child even into adulthood.

Filled with the Holy Spirit, speaking in tongues, given to discernment, prophecy, and interpretation, she was my perfect soulmate whom God had placed in my life. At many other times during church services, my congregants reported seeing angels standing behind me on the platform as I taught. When my wife and I stood together holding hands in the center aisle on Mother's Day, several women saw a bright glow surrounding us.

Several times during this first ministry, strange occult events occurred. One time, we experienced a man possessed by a demon, channeling a spirit. This happened during an evening service with a missionary from Africa. The demon spoke clearly from the mouth of this man who had a cleft palate and struggled with a severe speech impediment. My wife, the missionary and I prayed for him to be delivered, but the man refused and fled from the church.

Since I was new to this kind of spiritual encounter, I realized I needed to learn how to enter into spiritual warfare. I would sternly warn my young ministry couples to learn how to conduct spiritual warfare and be ready to engage.
Be spiritually aware and seek discernment of spirits. Be sensitive to the Holy Spirit for He will alert you to the enemy's presence. This Spiritual dimension is very real; demons are real. Satan and his angels are real and witchcraft is very much alive in the communities you will live in.

Be Obedient

My third word of encouragement is, to be obedient to the voice of the Lord. Before I ever knew the Lord, I heard the voice of the Lord. I somehow sensed, even as a nonbeliever, a voice speaking to me in dreams and in visions.

Normally, we would shop for kids' clothing for school paying with our credit card. However, we trusted the Lord. A day later, three of our neighbors stopped by. One gave us bags of clothes that their kids had outgrown. Many of them were brand new. A second person gave us bags of groceries and staples, and a third gave us men's and women's clothes.

God is so faithful. I can say without a doubt He has met and will meet every need you have. Just ask Him and be obedient when He says to do something even outrageous. He is the God of surprises, surplus and sustenance.

Most important – **Be Grateful!**

Not Everything in Ministry Is Serious
Roberta Anderson

One time in the Mifflinburg Assembly of God, I had left a space on the end of the pew for a friend to sit. One of the deacons came in, just saw my dark hair, sat down, and put his arm around my shoulders. Without looking and only seeing the dark hair, he thought I was his wife! Of course, the whole congregation started laughing and disrupted Bob's message.

Another time, I was playing the organ for song service and about six inches away, a mouse came out making a run for it on the heat duct! I kept playing and stifled a scream!

Chickens! Chickens! And More Chickens!
Ruby Mayeski

Throughout the years, God has been so faithful in meeting my needs. I'll never forget when we were serving our church in Illinois and my husband Richard Brinkman, was still going to seminary part-time, that our finances were tight. A church member called one day and said he would like to bring us some chickens for the freezer.

I was delighted! But when he came, he had forty LIVE chickens. He had bought them for twenty-three cents each at a sale. I had no idea how to pluck and clean a chicken or even cut up one. However, he graciously offered to help. He cut off their heads, and he and my husband plucked and cleaned them. Then, he taught me how to cut up the chicken, so we were blessed to have chicken to eat for many weeks.

Memorial Hearts in Sunshine
Barbara Recene

Our family life started in Sunshine, PA. This is where I met John. We were twelve and sixteen years old. We married in Sunshine, raised our children in Sunshine, and at the age of seventy-seven, John went to eternity in Sunshine. In between, we served many other places, but Sunshine was our sweet spot. Now my oldest daughter lives here in Sunshine with me. We make dinners for the church and serve others in need.

I have memorial hearts on the wall here in Sunshine. Pamela has many friends and family that tell her their best memories of our loved ones who have stepped into eternity. As they tell her the stories, Pamela doodles pictures inside a heart. Even I have learned stories I never knew. These memorial hearts are much better than a gravestone. They hang right here in my home where I am free to look at them and think of the many stories they represent. These hearts give me such comfort.

I live in the House of Abundance. There is much more to this story; the end is not nearly over yet. My favorite song is "Goodness of God" by Jenn Johnson. We have just begun.

Answering the Call to Missions
Becky Leake

In 2005, Jim's ninety-five-year-old aunt graduated to heaven. I remember as we traveled the turnpike to attend the funeral, we talked about resigning at Monroeville Assembly of God and entering another type of ministry. We both spoke of the people who attended the church and how we would miss our contact with missionaries and the ability to bless them financially. Our trip ended and we were back working at the church the next morning. I oversaw the Bible study for the women that morning. We were in a series called "The Lies Women Believe and the Truth That Sets Them Free." In the middle of the teaching, our leader stopped and said, "I don't know who this is for, but the Lord wants me to share this scripture." She opened to Jeremiah 31:14.

I opened the NIV Bible on my lap and read along with her. *"I will satisfy the priests with abundance. And my people will be filled with my bounty, declares The Lord."* I immediately thought that verse was for me.

In another version, it reads: *"The priests will enjoy abundance, and my people will feast on my good gifts. I, the Lord, have spoken!"* I went home that day and told Jim I believe the Lord has given us a promise. We had no idea how God would bring about the promise. As years went by, we have seen that promise fulfilled many times in our lives and the lives of needy pastors and people around the globe.

When we resigned, we didn't have one invitation to go to another country but soon we began to receive invitations. One came from Sri Lanka. Jim went to preach, but in the process, we met a pastor who had started an orphanage and had very little money. Sri Lanka had just suffered from a tsunami and they had many orphaned children. We didn't forget about them and we blessed the orphanage financially.

The scripture that our Bible study leader gave us began to be fulfilled. We received an invitation to go to Cuba. We were able to bless the pastors in Cuba with bathrooms, roofs on their homes, and back walls on their homes because they were flooded every time it rained. We gave gifts of jewelry for the women and money for the men. They were blessed with our gifts, but we were blessed with their commitment and dedication to God despite hardships and persecution.

We have blessed pastors in India, Nicaragua and Rwanda. Just recently, we received a report from Rwanda. It is a nation that has suffered genocide. One million people were murdered in three months. This was one of our most difficult mission trips. We toured a church that was turned into a museum of the genocide. They buried the bodies but kept all the clothing stacked on the pews. Ten thousand people were murdered there, but God is restoring and saving lives. We were able to bless a school led by believers with $7,000. The school had many Muslim students.

The people walked for miles to get dirty water to drink. Our most recent report told of pastors rejoicing about the 350 water filters they had received from us. Not only will it bless the pastor's family, but his village with clean water.

Praising God for His word and His promises.

Special People
Betty Martin

You're a special kind of people and
we're glad for you today,
We really wish to honor you in
a special kind of way.
We want to say a "Thank You"
for being what you are
If it were not for your kindness,
we would not get very far.

Who are these Special People?
Do you really want to know?
They're our senior citizens,
and we've learned to love them so.
Tho' it may seem down through the years
that you've been set aside

Yet there's a place for you today
To lead, to help, and to guide.
Because of all your patience, your love
and wisdom, too,
We serve this Savior better and
love Him just like you.

We need you, Special People
need you, yes, we do!
Tho' sometimes you may doubt it
Special People, we love you!

Ready to Meet Jesus!
Judy Kyllonen

I was born a little hillbilly girl in Corbin, Kentucky. My dad was an Assembly of God Minister and after being a pastor, he felt God call him to be an evangelist. After traveling for several years, our family of five settled in California. My dad started painting houses to supplement his income and began an affair with the lady whose house he was painting. He showed up with divorce papers and presented them to my mother. Now she had the responsibility of raising us three kids as a single parent.

My mother was very determined to be a fun-loving mother. She was also determined that all three of us kids would belong to Jesus and serve Him. She worked several jobs, in the school cafeteria, which God used to provide our supper each night. To this day, I do not like hot dogs!

After several years, my dad got his life straightened up and he was back in the ministry. He moved to Montana, where he had a ministry among the ranchers. He started a radio broadcast and called my mom asking for my sister, Joanna, and me to come and help him sing on the radio.

My mom agreed and put us on a Greyhound bus at the ages of eleven and twelve. We had to be at the radio station every morning at 6 a.m. to sing the theme song. He had rented an apartment underneath a tavern on skid row and every weekend we had a street meeting out in the front.

Joanna was always home from school before me and when I would come in the door, I would call, "Joanna, I'm home!" She would always answer me and say, "Okay!" One day I came home and called out my greeting and she didn't answer. I kept calling and still, nobody answered. And I called out, very loudly "OH NO, JESUS CAME AND I DIDN'T GO IN THE RAPTURE WITH HIM!"

I ran to my bedroom and I fell on my knees and cried out, "OH JESUS, PLEASE COME BACK AND GET ME!" This is when I heard, "Judy, I'm home!" I couldn't quit saying, "Thank you, Jesus! You haven't come for us yet!" For many, many years, since that experience, I have made sure that when Jesus comes, I WILL NOT BE LEFT BEHIND!

Angels vs. Bear - The Appalachian Trail
Vivian Dippold

In the fall of 2001, Otto and I enjoyed the outdoor treks into the wild. There were times when the "wild" became exactly that.

We had not been hiking or camping all summer because I had had a major twelve-hour brain surgery in late May. So, I was more than anxious to get back out on the trail. The days had shortened slightly, and a hint of coolness foretold of the coming season change. Yet, the heat of the midday created the right weather for an early fall backpacking trip on the great Appalachian Trail. Nothing could deter me from this trip.

We hiked through the pristine forest of the Delaware Water Gap heading to the High Point shelter. We passed sparkling lakes and rested on huge glacier boulders. By early evening, we spotted the trail marker: High Point lean-to - 0.5 m. Attached to the marker was a large sign cautioning that the bear population would be active. That simply meant walking heavily, talking loudly, hanging your food, or using the Bear Box (a metal secure box chained to the shelter). It was important not to eat near your tent and to clean up the area of all evidence of food. We knew all of this, so it was no problem.

The three-sided man-made shelter with a rough makeshift table and a wooden floor was set away from the trail. It was secluded among overhanging bushes and trees. A slight tremor engulfed me as I noticed trees with elongated scratches of bark on the trunks. The whole setting had a menacing look.

Closer inspection inside the shelter showed wooden posts had been gnawed, leaving what looked like the beginnings of a dugout canoe. On the table was a logbook with dates and names of people who had stopped there. The logbook documentation supported my growing uneasiness by offhandedly depicting a torrent of bear encounters:

"While sleeping in the shelter,
I woke up and found a bear breathing on my face."
"Woke up to a bear rummaging
through my backpack - gave it to him."

Additional entries all sounded the same. Wanting to sound brave, I endeavored to minimize the omens of danger.
"Whoever wrote all that stuff was probably just trying to spook anyone who came along. Make it sound really bad." You would think we would have moved on, but it was getting dark.

So, we opted for a grove of trees nestled about ten yards behind the shelter.

Anticipating every unseen event, Ott created a rope corral with the tent in the middle. I pushed aside any desire to know the details of this setup, but when he started stringing the pots and pans on the rope, I needed to know what he was doing. He explained that with the tent in the middle, ropes around it pans dangling from the rope, nothing would get past it without us knowing first. Hence, the first warning system was born.

After a camp stove meal, we leaned back in our camp chairs and enjoyed the enveloping darkness. I listened as the evening sounds play a musical background for the magnificent view of a full moon and clear starry sky. However, contrary to me and being the smart husband that he was, he did not share his uneasy feelings that the evening setting was becoming a curtain call of doom.

Later, zipped tightly within our domed tent, I slept while Ott listened to the disturbing night sounds. Finally, hours later, when he could take it no longer, he reached over and nudged me. I heard him exhale slowly and then a whisper. "Listen, a bear is in the shelter." It did not take long for me to hear the horrific banging and crashing that surrounded ominous. "How long has he been there?"

"A while, but he just started all that ruckus." Then with a deep muffled sigh, he whispered, "Maybe he'll just go away."

I quietly added, "We can hope." The sounds outside the tent portrayed a bear searching for something or someone. Surely God did not bring my life through that surgery to have it end here.

A dismal headline appeared in my mind: *Pots on a Rope Encompass Spot Where Couple was Eaten by a Bear.*

Our glow-in-the-dark watches indicated that we had several hours to wait before daylight. Without moving and barely breathing, we silently prayed, confessed to any overlooked sin, and pleaded to our Creator for our lives. The tirade continued until about 6 a.m. when the audible performance stopped. We quietly unzipped the tent flap and this courageous wilderness team peaked into the semi-lit surroundings.

Remembering that loud noises can scare bears away, we got the aluminum mess kits from our packs. On the count of three, a banging filled the morning air. It definitely got the attention of Mr. High Point Bear. From the shelter came a horrendous growl and a thunderous charge. Frozen, we watched as he headed straight toward the tent. But unbelievable as it may seem, about six feet from our tent, one very large bear took a 90° turn and shot off into the woods. He was never seen again - at least not by us.

"No disaster will come near your tent. For he will command his angels concerning you to guard you in all your ways." Psalm 91:10-11(NIV). It surely must've been those angels.

On a quick assessment of the shelter, we found Mr. Bear had eaten part of the makeshift log table. Then I added a hasty emphatic note in the logbook. "Bear ate the table - no kidding! Don't sleep in this shelter." It took five minutes to pack up camp and head down the trail. Breakfast could wait.

Our Missions Trip to Trinidad
Ruby Mayeski

My husband Anthony and I loved to be with our family members. One year we took a trip to Trinidad and Tobago to visit our missionary son Sam and his wife Jan. We thoroughly enjoyed the beauty of the islands, the wonderful boat ride, and the delicious meals. But the greatest thrill of all was to experience the joyous worship services where the people praised the Lord with all their hearts. Their lives were so fragrant with the beauty of the Lord. No matter their cultural, social or economic differences, they lived together in wonderful harmony and unity. They reached out with great compassion to the lost and the hurting. To me, it was an example of what the early Church must have been like, as well as an example for us today.

When The Lord Heals, He Heals for Life
Jean Tennant

My husband Chester and I spent thirty-four years pioneering churches throughout the Appalachian District. I know what it means to work hard for the Kingdom of God. It wasn't easy, but it was fulfilling!

I have experienced the healing hand of God so many times throughout our ministry. When our son Stephen was a baby he had baronial pneumonia. Doctors were not expecting him to live through the three-mile drive to the nearest hospital. But, God spared his life.

Several years back I had to have hip surgery leaving me unable to bend my knee. The doctors told me it would never get better. One evening after service I was prayed for by a visiting minister. I began to hear a grinding sound. Before I knew it, I was able to bend my knee without pain. To this day I have had no problems with it. When the Lord heals, He heals for life!

God's Word kept me going as I came to realize that *"I can do all things through Christ who strengthens me."*

A Woman's Touch
Sharon Shimko
This article was written by Sharon Bremigen Shimko
*And published in Women's Touch * Nov/Dec 1989*

It's Christmastime. When we hear that word, many of us feel a wave of nostalgia usually accompanied by an image of contentment. We see, in our mind's eye, rosy-cheeked children in soft pajamas snuggled peacefully in their cozy, warm beds.

We see softly lit rooms, transformed by the glow of candlelight and the twinkling of a tree. Beyond the visual joys is the aroma of sweet and spicy goodies piled high on racks until cool enough to place in festive containers.

Presents are beautifully wrapped, tied with matching bows, and placed around the tree.

Each day brings joyous greetings from friends and relatives making our hearts grateful for the blessings of being loved and the happiness of loving in return.

But let's go beyond the ideal. Let's look at Christmas with realism.

Frequently, bedtime for those cherubs can be anything but peaceful. Who saw that their pajamas were clean and cuddly-soft and that those cheeks were rosy and not smeared with the jelly that sneaked out of the edge of a hastily prepared sandwich?

What artist transformed those everyday rooms into rooms that glowed with the sights of lights of this festive season?

Who fills the house with the tantalizing aroma of Christmas goodies? Who makes sure relatives and friends receive greetings of the season that say, "With love from our house to your house"?

By now you probably have the idea. It's you, the woman, the homemaker.

Christmas can be hard work, but when December comes, extra jobs are squeezed into an already hectic week. A grocery budget, already extended by double coupons and refunds, stretches to include chocolate chips, candied fruits, and extra flour.

Why all these preparations? Could it be as we transform our homes into holiday places, that somehow our hearts and minds are transformed by the real message of Christmas?

Christmas is love. For God so loved the world that He gave. Jesus so loved that He came. As women, we have a kind of love that nurtures, gives, and provides. It's a love sometimes described as the woman's touch.

Many years ago, Mary must have prepared in the best way possible for the birth of her child. She dealt with the reality of life, not believing she deserved the ideal though she was pregnant with the Son of God. She knew how to stretch a budget to include a new baby, an unexpected trip, and an inconvenient tax.

She knew what it was like to have less than ideal surroundings in which to have her baby. Her realities were stark, bare boards and the apprehension of giving birth for the first time.

Yes, I believe the lowly stable was transformed by God's love that night, but I also believe it was filled with the nurturing, giving love of a woman.

At this beautiful and blessed time of the year, become like Mary. Allow God to transform first your heart, then your surroundings into places filled with love -- the true reality of Christmas.

What Is Death?
Rev. Betty Schell

What is death? It is a door! That opens wide to all.
Our days are numbered since our birth, The very old to small.

What is death? It is a door! That leads to eternity.
It will not end, it is a friend, It's designed for you and me.

What is death? It is a door! To live beyond this life.
Void of fears, death, and tears, To where there is no strife.

What is death? It is a door! Do not fear to enter.
'Twill be a life of greatest joy, A walk of glorious splendor.

What is death? It is a door! I'll leave all struggling behind.
My fight with sin, the victory win A new life I now find.

What is death? It is a door! Oh death, where is thy sting?
The grave gave up its victory, The bells of heaven ring!

Carols Christmas Blessing
Carol Kenzy

It was 1947 and I celebrated Christmas in Los Angeles, CA, with my older brother and parents. My Dad was a full-time Bible school student, holding down three jobs to provide for his family. Christmas was coming, and Paul and I were SO excited.

Our parents asked us what we wanted for Christmas. Paul answered, "a bike." I quickly responded, "a trike." These were impossible dreams for a struggling family of four. We were gently reminded that we needed to pray and ask Jesus to hear and answer our prayers, as He was our Provider. And pray we did . . . as only two children could . . . with unvarnished faith!

The next day, a friend casually asked my Dad, "Hey, Glen do you know anyone who needs a bicycle and a tricycle?" Dad was overwhelmed by this almost-immediate answer to prayer. He painted these precious gifts, added new accessories, and with thanksgiving, placed them under the tree.

Imagine our joy when we saw the answer to our prayers on Christmas morning! Not only did the Lord answer our prayers, but He also laid a foundation of faith in our six-year-old and four-and-a-half-year-old's hearts. That's why I've been able to trust Him in all things for over fifty-five years in ministry! Truly, Carol's Christmas Blessing was not merely a tricycle, it was a faith-filled lesson that has lasted a lifetime. For that, I am eternally grateful!

As we trust Him for the unknowns ahead, His plans for us are for good and not for evil. Jeremiah 29:11. (NIV) *"For I know the plans I have for you," says the Lord, "plans to prosper you and not to harm you, plans to give you hope and a future."* That means the answer may be Yes, No or Wait. We can't improve on His plans!

How China and Africa Came Together
Rev. Evelyn Bolton

Being raised in a Christian missionary family in South Africa, I learned to love the Lord as a child. Pentecost was not unknown to me. While alone at home one evening I seriously began seeking for the baptism in the Holy Spirit. After much surrender and commitment, my pursuit was not in vain.

During my first year at Central Bible College, I met my husband Robert. He was the Missionary Band president and led the Friday night missionary service. I was most surprised when asked to be his date to the GPH (Gospel Publishing House) missionary banquet held each year to get GPH personnel more acquainted with missionary students at Central Bible Institute.

This is how an MK (missionary's kid) from China got together with an MK from Africa, which in due time formed an "Afro-Asian Alliance."

Advice and Encouragement from My Mother
Written by the daughter of Joy Bolton Kelly

As we entered the mission field and said goodbye to my mother, it brought back so many memories of her farewells and she lived quite a few!

She, as a young girl, said farewell to her family in Africa as her ship slowly left the port for America. She saw her home country getting smaller and fainter on the horizon. Then there were the comings and goings as she and dad served on the mission field of Taiwan, which included me and my sister. Years later there were the farewells as she and dad left grown and married children behind as they continued to serve where God had called them. Now the farewells included their precious grandchildren knowing they'd miss much of their growing up years. Add to that having me and my husband also going on the mission field, separating our families further. This was a family of farewells because now a granddaughter would leave for the mission field! *(But it was only an earthly farewell.)*

My wise mother gave some wonderful advice:

- One of the "gems" she told my husband and me when we were starting out was, "When dealing with difficult people, you must be thick-skinned, not thick-headed!"
- Don't be so quick to take offense, but to sift criticism wisely.

- Be humble enough to let good advice penetrate; even if the way it's imparted is hard to take.
- Don't limit yourself to what you think is your "own" abilities. If you're a quiet and timid person like I was, you'll be surprised what God can do in your life if you let Him.
- SUBMIT, COMMIT, AND LET GOD DO IT!
- Minister alongside your husband because your ministries complement each other. Your marriage can be an example to a troubled world.
- Another "gem" was, when concerned for my safety, she had to surrender me, her adult daughter, to the mission field. She told me the Lord imparted to her that "the safest place to be is in the center of His will."

There Are Always Blessings in Obedience
Evelyn Machamer

> "God will always bless you as long as you are obedient. Do what He tells you to do, no matter how strange it may seem."

A Funny Memory
Rev. Connie Homerski

One night, my son Tim drove me and his younger brothers to an old church out in the country. We all went to the front pew to sit down. All of a sudden, we heard a horrible cracking sound. The pew collapsed to the floor! We still laugh about it to this day!

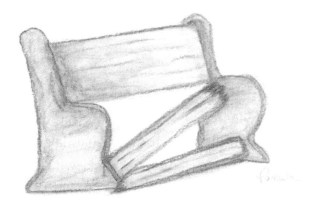

He Touched Me
Lorraine Swank

In 1952, Jim and I were students at EBI (Eastern Bible Institute/University of Valley Forge), and the Asian flu was rampant, affecting a great number of the students. Since we were married and living in a cottage on campus, we were not sick until later when I began to experience all the symptoms. I was confined to my bed for several weeks and couldn't keep anything down and lost a lot of weight.

Previously, I had been praying and wanting to learn more about true faith. When I became sick, I had a strong compelling desire to trust God completely. I had never before, or since, had such a mighty determination to totally trust God to do whatever He wanted with me. I refused to see a doctor; I was fully content to let God have His way. Really, I did not care whether I lived or died. It was whatever He decided was my goal. It was wonderful to feel that confidence and trust in Jesus that could not be shaken. Jim was being told by his elders that he could be in trouble with the law if I died without a doctor's attention. Still, I was not moved. (I have been to the doctor many times in my life down through the years.)

I did not know it yet, but I had become pregnant before I got the flu. Jim felt overwhelmed with all of this and decided that he would fast and pray until I was healed. That day, he went to English class. Each class was always opened with prayer and Miss Wedding asked him to pray. When he had prayed, she said, "I feel that we should pray for Brother Swank and the burden he is carrying and for others who are still sick. "The entire class began to intercede and spent the remainder of the class time praying."

When Jim came home from class that day, I asked him if he would get me some Alka-Seltzer. I drank it and vomited violently. Then I asked for some buttermilk (which I really didn't like). He went and got it for me. I drank it, kept it down, and slept for a while. Later that evening, I asked for a ham sandwich and a chocolate milkshake. He ran next door and told Sister VanMeter what I wanted, and she said, "Give that girl anything she asks for!"

He went to the store, bought the ingredients, and made them for me. I ate them and kept them down! I was soon out of bed and going about my duties.

I look back on it all now and realize God gave me cravings for what I needed to clean out my system and heal it and for the food that I needed. Also, I learned that after you have been without food for such a long time, a ham sandwich and chocolate milkshake are not the way to start eating again. It was God's healing in my body. I was rejoicing in what God did in my body and my spirit.

Later that year, God blessed us with a very healthy baby girl, Kerri. I saw Sister VanMeter many years later and she inquired about Kerri's health. Sister VanMeter had done some nursing during the flu epidemic during WWI. She told me that they were never able to save any pregnant women who also had the flu.

What a powerful experience with the Lord! I will never forget what God did for me!

Unexpected Miracles
Mari Lynn Richter

God does miracles when we don't expect them. When my husband was in graduate school, we had two small children at that time, a baby and a toddler. We had absolutely no money for food. God said He would provide and He did. We had been to church and came home to find grocery bags full of food. The Word says that He knows what we have need of before we even ask.

Our first church was a small home missions church. I think there was a total of ten people. There were two main families in the church. One family was very faithful. The other came and went and was gone again, as the wind blows. Because of the continual tension between the families and the financial stress of keeping the church open, the District felt it best to close the church. We agreed and the District said we could live in the parsonage that was attached to the church for a month. The first Sunday, there was knocking on the door.

As we opened the door, a young couple stood before us with two children and asked what time our services started. We invited them in had coffee and shared with them. They asked if they could meet the next Sunday. We met and there were more people. By the end of the month (with adults and children in attendance) there were close to thirty individuals worshipping on Sunday. We approached the District with this new outcome and the church resumed and grew.

As the months moved forward, a new couple started attending, but the husband was an alcoholic and was known in the community as the "town drunk." One Sunday morning as my husband gave the altar call, this man walked forward, knelt and was saved. From that day forward, he never took another drink. God had delivered him, saved him and his family by the blood of Christ. He was redeemed. In the future, he then became known as the "town evangelist." He shared his testimony wherever he went.

The church that was positioned to close had become a lighthouse to the community.

How I Came into Pentecost
Rev. Thomas Hamilton

In my early childhood years, my parents attended the Oak Ridge Union Church in Oak Ridge, PA. This was a non-denominational church, pastored by Rev. Harold Goss. It was during that time a couple by the name of Homer and Dot Phrop came to the area holding revival services in the small school auditorium. Homer taught about the baptism in the Holy Spirit. My parents, Tom and Dora, attended that revival service with us children.

On our way home, I was seated in the front seat with my parents and my dad turns to my mom and says, "Dora, I think it's real." My mom replied, "I will find out." The next day, after my dad went off to work in the coal mines, my mom said, "Kids, I want you to go next door to play."

We asked, "How long can we stay?" Her reply, "As long as you want to." Usually, we could only play for a half-hour at a time. On this particular day, mom had something to do.

My mom got down on her knees and began praying. The end result of the afternoon was that mom was filled with the Holy Spirit. My dad came home at 4 o'clock to find my mom standing in the kitchen doorway with a smile on her face.

Dad walked up to mom and said, "Something happened to you today." My mom's reply was simply, "It's real!" My mom embraced my dad, who was covered from head to toe in coal dust and began speaking in tongues.

My dad tried to reason with the pastor of the Union Church, but he didn't get to first base. Harold Goss kept telling my dad, "Tom, it's not for today."

Nevertheless, on Sunday morning my parents along with their five children filled one whole row at the Oak Ridge Union Church. As the pastor began to speak, he managed to weave into his message: "The baptism in the Holy Spirit is NOT for today."

At that, my dad stood to his feet and moved into the center aisle. He turned to the whole family and motioned with his finger for us to rise and follow him. We rose and followed my dad to the exit door of the church.

While we were walking out the pastor calls out, "Tom, I'd like to speak with you." My Dad replied by saying, "Howard, it's too late." My family walked out. Later on, my dad and Howard had a long discussion and Dad never budged. Many years later, that same church invited my dad's son, Thomas (me), back to preach a Pentecostal message. The results of that message led to a prayer line that lasted for several hours.

The Man of Few Shoes
Vivian Dippold

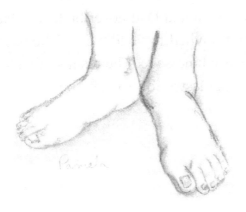

It's amusing the things I remember within the circle of our 51 years together. Ott was humorous; he would always find a way to make me laugh – well, most of the time! Here is where it started.

June 10, 1967 "Hey, you like my new shoes?"

I looked at him curiously but lovingly. My gaze dropped and sure enough at the bottom of those long tux-draped legs were new black leather shoes. I glanced up and silently acknowledged the success. I added a big smile, then quickly shifted my gaze back to the minister standing in front of us. I realized the significance of the moment. Since he always found it difficult to find shoes that really fit comfortably, this was monumental. This was important. They were great-looking shoes. I was so glad he was able to find a pair in time. I had worried about that.

"We are gathered here in the sight of God to unite Otto and Vivian…". My challenge of outfitting this handsome guy with appropriate shoes had begun.

Over the years, I'd have to say his favorite footwear were boots…cowboy boots…barn boots. The job of being an assistant director of a Christian-based ranch for troubled youth allowed these boots, or should I say, it was mandated. The ranch was filled with a gazoodle of boys and about twelve or more horses (can't remember exactly). Ott would take the boys, as well as our own children, on trail rides and teach them the skills of caring for the horses. Those boots were covered with dirt, straw and manure. They were the best.

Then, it wasn't long before those boots were changed to steel-toed boots as he became the contractor, building a needed educational facility for the boys. This was a renaissance man. He did the work, putting down footers, laying blocks, assembling walls and roofs. He would always say, "If there was a job to be done that a man can do, I am a man. I can do it." And he did.

But on Sundays, the grunge, cement and dirt were left behind as this man put on a suit, tie and comfortable-fitting Sunday shoes. He played the trumpet, led worship, and preached. Well, not all at the same time, but over the course of years, each of those jobs were earnestly filled by the Man of Few Shoes.

Years flew by and soon those feet took on hiking boots and covered so many miles searching for pristine lakes, snow-capped mountains, desert trails and roaring rivers. However, the trails became less traveled as medical problems became the issue. Chemo and radiation, while attempting to kill cancer cells, left him with neuropathy in both feet. The difficulty of finding suitable shoes became impossible. Walking was a struggle. Even sitting brought pain that could not be cured.

Now, in a lonely closet sits one pair of each: Sunday shoes, cowboy boots, sandals and sneakers all empty and dusty. No more struggle to find the right fit. No more struggle to make walking tolerable. At this point, I'm not sure if there are even shoes on his feet. Now he walks on the streets of transparent glass in the City of Gold (Revelation 21:20). But one thing is for sure, there is now no longer the problem of getting the shoes to fit comfortably.

I Loved to Sing
Hattie Grazier

Before I went to Bible school I worked for the NJ Bell Telephone Company as a telephone operator. My husband Hobart and I were married in 1949. After he finished his educational studies, we pastored at Bethel Tabernacle in South Philadelphia for five years.

During my college years at EBI (Eastern Bible Institute), I was a soloist in the traveling choir and was chosen to be the soloist for graduation. Before having a stroke in 2007, I traveled with a group for three years singing in churches and other organizations. I have learned that if I wait upon the Lord, He will renew my strength; so, I will mount up on wings as eagles; run and not be weary; walk and not faint.

"O the depth of the riches both of the wisdom and knowledge of God! How unsearchable are his judgments, and his ways past finding out!" Romans 11:33

I Was Railroaded!
Jeanne Myers

The date was August 20, 1941. The place was the dance floor at Benny's Place in New Providence. That's where my husband John and I met for the first time. I had come with a date, but John was determined to dance with me. So, he arranged a special dance that would assure we would end up together and we did! A month later we had our first date. By Christmas, we were engaged and we married on January 31, 1942.

Two years later we gave our hearts to Jesus and two months after that I found myself living on campus at Eastern Bible Institute, Green Lane, PA. I was railroaded!

How We Met
Jennie Bedzyk

In the late 1800s, my parents came to America in search of a better life. What they found was Jesus!

I was introduced to my husband Peter during an evangelistic meeting. Peter was the evangelist. After the meetings ended, he continued traveling and ministering the Gospel in many churches throughout Pennsylvania.

For some time, we wrote back and forth as he traveled. I was twenty-seven and he was thirty when we married. For over fifty years we ministered in the Penndel District. During our last twenty-six years together we ministered to the seniors at First Assembly of God in Erie, PA.

What Are You Seeking?
Rev. Ted Graobski

Before I came to the Lord, I was listening to a sermon by a Franciscan Friar. He was preaching on Matthew 6:33 and asked the question, "What are you seeking?" This shook me to my very core.

I received Jesus at the age of twenty-seven when I was a student in Athens, Georgia. A year later I was filled with the Holy Spirit at a Charismatic Prayer Conference.

I met my future wife Kathy Gioia in 1987 at a Wednesday night church service. She was leading the worship. I proposed to her a few months later and I took her on our first official date to New York for dinner and a play. Ten months later we were married.

The Train Ride
Rev. James Mugford

I was born and raised in a home where we faithfully attended the local Assembly of God church. However, just going to church with my family did not change the way I lived my life. It wasn't until I was seventeen that God really spoke to my heart and put a call of ministry on my life.

In the fall of 1948, I took the train from Boston, Massachusetts to CBI (Central Bible Institute) in Springfield, MO. In 1950, I met my future wife Ruth Bittel. We were married in December 1951.

Meeting at The Water Cooler
Jayne Grove

At the age of fourteen, I gave my heart to Jesus.

I met my husband James at the company where we both worked. One day, I needed some heavy string and was told he had some in his office. We met at the water cooler. He asked if he could walk with me on my way home that evening. The next day several girls told me that he said, "Wow, she roped me in." Twenty months later, we were married.

I could write a book of God's provisions over the years. Years ago, I suffered from migraine headaches. On December 4, 1975, while sitting in my living room, praising and worshipping God, I felt the Lord touch me. I have never had another headache.

Note: *Jayne served as the PennDel Women's Ministry Director from 1980 to 1996. God laid a strong burden on her heart for the widows of the PennDel Ministry Network. She shared her burden with Marlene Martin and the More Than Conquerors Ministry was born.*

More Than a Brother
Rev. Milford Watters

At the age of eighteen, I was serving in the Navy. One day while on the beach in Gulfport, MS, I was picked up by my future wife Linda, her sister and three others who witnessed to me. Two weeks later, I accepted Jesus as my Lord.

Linda and I became like brother and sister, while I was dating her sister Helen. Soon after breaking up with Helen, I realized that I was more than just a "brother" to Linda...the rest is history!

While in North East Bible School, I was a Youth Pastor in Perkasie, PA, and during my senior year, I became pastor of Grace Chapel, Green Lane, PA. I pastored there for four years.

The best verse to describe what Jesus has done for me and who I am today is Galatians 2:20

"I have been crucified with Christ and I no longer live, but Christ lives in me. The life I now live in the body, I live by faith in the Son of God, who loved me and gave himself for me."

His Greatest Compliment
Carolyn Leeper

One of the greatest compliments my husband gave me before he passed away was, "No matter what I had to do or where I had to go, you were always there for me and encouraged me to keep going." There were times when our children were small that I could not go along with him, but I prayed for him to be able to accomplish God's will in whatever situation he had to handle.

God will never leave us or put us in a situation that we cannot handle, but He will give us the strength and courage to accomplish His work.

Heaven's Hounds
Lorraine Swank

We were pastoring in Lansdale, PA, and had scheduled a service with Brother Scotti, a missionary. It was February and a big snow hit us on the very night that the missionary was to come. He did come, and we had a service as scheduled. I was contemplating what a meager offering the few folks would be able to give, I was talking to Jesus saying how I wished that I had something to give. You see, my wallet was empty…except for a small "stash."

Jesus, who sees all and knows all reminded me of the $5.00 stashed in my secret compartment. I argued with Him, "That is money that You have provided for the kid's shoes. You know how they have grown out of their shoes!" But Jesus did not accept my reasoning or excuse and kept "hounding" me. After all, I had prayed for shoe money and He had provided it. Finally, offering time came. I surrendered to the Lord and dug out my $5.00 putting it in the offering plate.

The next Sunday, I was sitting in church with eleven-month-old Glenn on my lap. With my head bowed and eyes closed as we were praying, I felt someone press something into my hand. I immediately opened my eyes because many times folks would give me a note or prayer request to give to the pastor. It was not a note. I saw that it was money!

So, I looked around to see if I could learn who had put it in my hand. There was a little old lady, who came from Highway Home for the Aged, returning to her seat a few rows behind me! I do not remember her name, but I will never forget her deed! I wondered if Jesus had to "hound" her as He did me?

After the service, as we were driving home and I was telling Jim about it, I reached into my pocket for the precious gift that she had placed in my hand. NO, it was not a "payback" of the $5.00 I had given. It wasn't even double that amount; it was six times what I had given in the missionary offering! It was $30.00. Not only could I buy shoes for the kids, but I got much-needed shoes for myself and I still had money left over. (That happened in 1957.)

WOW! It surely works out gloriously to be obedient to Heaven's Hound! Greater than the money is the blessing and learning through it all. PTL!

The Cattle on a Thousand Hills
Mari Lynn Richter

When my husband and I were pastoring our first church, there was an evangelist holding revival services at a neighboring church. We knew the pastors and I really felt we should go.
My husband and I agreed to get the "chores" done so we could go. I would mow the lawn and he would do his sermon preparation.

Then, we realized that we had no money for gas and the church was not able to pay us. I remember praying, "God, you own all the cattle on a thousand hills and one of those cows is ours." I had no doubt that God would meet our needs.

My husband siphoned gas from the lawnmower to put into the gas tank of the car so we could drive thirty miles to the revival. We attended the service. After the service when people were leaving, the evangelist called to us and said: "This couple I do not know, but they have a need."

We were blessed with a collection of $119.00. Filling the gas tank and paying our bills was exactly $119.00. God never fails.

The Desires of our Heart
Mary Harman

I know from many experiences that God knows our desires and needs. I've found that He provides these many times. Back in the 1970s, with help, John built a four-bedroom parsonage and we needed furniture. A small church in Michigan had given us a Christmas gift, and with it, John bought us a coffee table. The next year, we looked at the same store for matching end tables, but they didn't have them. The following year, we didn't have the money to even look for additional furniture, but I still wanted matching end tables.

By the next year, that particular kind was out of style and no one carried them. I continued watching the newspaper for those end tables. Finally, there were end tables listed and, after holding the ad for two weeks, I finally called. They were still available. I took a drawer over to see if they might be a close match.

To my surprise - a miracle - they were the exact match as the two we had bought many years ago. No one can ever make me doubt that God has provided. He gave me the desire of my heart.
Even in the material needs, He delights in answering prayer requests.

Yard sales were my delight in finding just what I needed - even clothes for my family.

Yesterday, Today, Tomorrow
Rev. Sylvia Baker

Hebrews 13:6-7 (CSB) *"So we say with confidence, I will not be afraid. What can man do to me? Remember your leaders who spoke the word of God to you. Consider the outcome of their way of life and imitate their faith. Jesus Christ is the same yesterday, today, and forever."*

Yesterday

I was raising kids and working hard. Looking back, I have experienced a lot of yesterdays. Some great – some not so great. My husband traveled a lot for his job and my mother didn't live nearby. My grandmother lived with us and so I was able to contribute to our finances. I worked for consulting engineers as an administrative manager and was blessed to travel throughout the US setting up new offices.

Today

I am more than blessed to be sharing God's Word. I came to the Shanksville Assembly of God from Pitcairn Assembly of God. I have been able to share His Word for 26 years. Since completing all the necessary schooling, the people I have worked with and worked for have all helped me to learn and grow in my own walk with the Lord.

Tomorrow

I have returned to the Pittsburgh area. My daughter Susan and her husband Mark have graciously made room for me and my cat! I now have new opportunities to share with folks in this area. However, I already miss being in the pulpit. God has been so good to me and He continues to make a way for me!

Bits About Our Lives
Rev. Betty Schell

I became a Christian in 1947, when I was eleven years old, at an Open Bible Church in Westville, NJ. I entered Eastern Bible Institute (EBI) where I met Walter. He was in his last year of college, and I was in my first year, which became my last year. I got my "MRS" degree!

The first place we ministered was at Oxford, PA. We were there for about ten months.

It was held in a former jewelry store. God provided our financial needs at our first several churches by Walter working part-time and with the help of our parents. We did not get a salary from these churches but were provided the parsonage and utilities.

I praise God that He has given me a very healthy body. I have only suffered from minor things throughout my life.

A funny story to share: While pastoring the Assembly of God church in Philipsburg, PA, my second son, then four years old, wanted me to see the silly sink over at the church. We lived next to the church and, as we entered the church, it dawned on me that he was referring to the urinal in the men's room!

I have held "Chalk Talk" meetings on "Jesus is the Light of the World." I would share a message and then draw a lighthouse while a CD played with John Starnes singing, "The Lighthouse."

The Reality of Hell
Rev. David Selleck

At the age of six or seven, I became quite ill. During that time God began to speak to my heart. In a dream, I was overwhelmed with the sense that I was falling into Hell. I let out a scream as I fell off the couch onto the floor and woke up.

It wasn't until my mid-teens that I knelt by an old chair, with a torn leather seat, as my altar. Soaking it with tears of remorse for putting God off so long, I surrendered my life to follow Christ in a small Sullivan Street Mission in Elmira, NY.

He Is There
Rev. Grace Hardt

When I need a word of comfort, He is there!
When I struggle 'neath the burden, He is there!
When the blue skies turn to gray,
And I cannot find my way
At the closing of the day, He is there!

When I cannot face tomorrow, He is There!
When my life is filled with sorrow, He is there!
When I dread the coming dawn,
And it seems I can't go on
When my hope is almost gone, He is there!
Jesus said, "I will not leave you comfortless."

Financial Provision
Rev. Lawane Hahn

When I was young, I attended Oral Roberts healing services. I had just accepted Christ and had no knowledge of sowing and reaping at that time. In one of the services, my wife and I heard that, if we pledged one hundred dollars, we would receive three times that amount. I felt led to give the money, but I didn't even have it at the time.

In that year, my place of employment had a Christmas meal for their employees. I received an envelope at the dinner. Later that night when I opened it, there was exactly three hundred dollars.

I began learning and growing in the faith, but I still wasn't tithing. Even though we weren't giving financially, God was taking care of us. The place that I was working went out of business and I was out of a job. At this time, I was offered two different jobs, and I also heard about another job that was a possibility. I began to pray about which job, I should take. The Lord led me to take the right job, because later I found that the other two places that offered me a job went out of business.

During this time, I began to seriously consider tithing, but fear was holding me back. Each month we would run out of money, but I was ready to take this step. I discussed this with my wife and she encouraged me to do what I felt God wanted. After the first month of tithing, we actually had money left over after paying all the bills. Shortly after this, I received the largest raise of any part's manager and was told I was the most productive employee in the auto department. Over the next three years, my wages tripled.

Years later, one of my sons wanted to attend the Christian school at our church. We transported them to school and were reimbursed for the mileage driven. Not only was the gas covered, but there was enough money left to pay for my children's tuition. God is surely our provider.

Search Me, O God
Lorraine Swank

We experienced a wonderful revival, totally inspired by the Holy Spirit, in our youth group in Moosic, PA. As my husband Jim spoke to the group about some issues that were not pleasing to the Lord, the young people listened and responded to what the Holy Spirit was saying to them individually.

That meeting climaxed with a precious altar service where individuals asked for forgiveness and gave forgiveness to each other. Some were filled with the Holy Spirit. We prayed and worshiped for quite a long time. Parents were calling the church asking where their kids were! My memory says that it was about midnight before we dismissed them that night.

That atmosphere kept up in all our CA services for a year or more - off and on. (Youth groups in those days were called CAs - Christ Ambassadors.) They were bringing their friends, who were getting saved. Our numbers grew making it necessary to move the CA services from our original smaller space to the sanctuary.

I was blessed to experience the many changes that God made in all our lives. That fall, a total of six students went off to various Bible Colleges. I continue to treasure and be grateful for the memories of how those young people loved to spend so much time praying and rejoicing in Jesus!

TO GOD BE THE GLORY!

The Drunk Down the Street
Mari Lynn Richter

There was a family who lived down the road from us and the man was always drunk. One day he came over to our house and, as always, he was drunk. He told my husband, "I want you to come over (on such a day) at 10:00 a.m. because I need to talk to you and, by that time, I will be sober."

The day came and at 10:00 a.m. my husband went over to visit this neighbor. He was sober and he had his mother's Bible on the table. He poured coffee and sat down. He said, "I want you to tell me how to be saved." My husband went through the "Romans Road" with him. Finally, my husband asked if this drunk wanted to ask Jesus into his heart. The man said, "Yes." With tears streaming down his face, he said "The Sinner's Prayer."

We didn't see him in church, but God knows the heart. When we left that church, we found out that the man had suddenly died from an aneurysm in the brain. God knew his heart.

Kid's Camp
Mary Harmon

I have always loved camps growing up. My family lived in Braeside, Ontario. During a kid's service, I gave my heart to Jesus and was filled with the Holy Spirit. In those days, the buildings were made of wood and the ground was straw. No glass windows. Good memories.

John retired from pastoring on August 31, 2005. They were having difficulty finding counselors at the kid's camp I used to attend. I volunteered to work as a counselor which surprised other counselors because I was in my 70s. One night, with auditorium lights low, we were all praying on the floor at the altar. I felt someone had a hand on my shoulder. Thinking it was a counselor, I turned to thank her. I was stunned to see a beautiful blonde-haired, blue-eyed girl smiling at me. Then she said, "GOD IS STILL GOING TO USE YOU." She again repeated it.

I said, "Honey, did you know I am a pastor's wife and that my husband has resigned. As of now, we have no home to go to and, of course, I'm anxious about the future." She replied, "No, I didn't know." I went on to thank her for letting the Holy Spirit use her to encourage me.

The next day, I found out her name was Katie and that she had told her counselor about what she said to me. The counselor asked her, "Who told you to tell her that?" She simply said, "God did."

It's so important to pour into our kids God's Word and our love. Only God knows the plans for each and every one of these kids. Yes, the Holy Spirit, can work in their lives and can speak through them.

The Story of My Life
Roberta Anderson

I was in Pentecost before I was born and came to know Jesus when I was six or seven years old. My grandfather had been a circuit-riding Methodist minister and became an Assemblies of God minister. I spent many nights sleeping on a pew as we had services: Sunday morning, Sunday night, Tuesday night, and Thursday night. Plus, there might have been services in between.

Bob and I met when we were about twelve years old when his grandmother brought him to church. He would walk me to the bus stop after CA (Christ's Ambassadors) meetings. Then, we lost contact until he was in the Navy and his grandmother asked me to write to him as he was on a six-month cruise in the Mediterranean Sea. He proposed in a letter three months later and we were married eight months after that.

We were first at Wilmington First Assembly of God as an assistant pastor. Then our first church was in Mifflinburg, PA, where we ministered for eight years. I've always believed God would supply our needs, but one time it was so totally unexpected that I could hardly believe it.

Bob was in the hospital in Salisbury, MD. A couple from our church paid for me to stay in a hotel for ten days across from the hospital so that I wouldn't have to drive back and forth. Then, the doctors said he would have to stay three more days.

I knew I didn't have the money to stay and was feeling a little down. I went into the hotel restaurant for supper and sat down at a table next to another table where a lady was reading. Since I am a reader, I asked what she was reading and we started talking. She asked why I was there, and I told her Bob was in the hospital and would have to be there three more days.

She asked if I was going to stay three more days and I told her, "No, I can't afford it." She said that I would be staying and that she would pay for it. She also paid for my meal. Turned out that she and her husband were Christians who attended a Baptist church in Virginia. They didn't want to be thanked and wouldn't give me their address. God really works in mysterious ways. Doesn't He?

There have always been different miracles in my life, but one was that I got to meet my biological father in 2000 and gained a whole new family. He died in 2001, so it was a miracle that I had a year to get to know him.

Upstate NY in the Adirondack Mountains
Rowann Rainbow

It was in the resort area of the Adirondacks of New York that I became familiar with Pentecost. My parents rented a cottage from May to September. They made many friends and the most wonderful thing was that we were surrounded by Christians. There were adult camps, youth camps and children's camps every summer.

As I was growing up, I could have great fellowship in activities and worship which was special to me and my walk with the Lord.

The adults would have devotions in our living room every morning. The presence of the Lord was so real. I began to feel what Pentecost was all about.

During the fall and winter, we would attend Pentecostal prayer meetings in homes near us. Our families became close and each desired a special dedication for their children. I became good friends with one of the girls and we sang together. God had His plan for my life.

A new pastor came into our area and my family began to attend the church. They were without a pianist and found out I played, so I accepted the opportunity. I became acquainted with the pastor's son and we started to date. After he graduated from high school, he attended Bible college.

Our desire was to minister for the Lord. After three years, my husband-to-be graduated and was praying for God to lead us. He received an invitation to accept a church off the Outer Banks of North Carolina on an island called Ocracoke, which was unknown to either of us. He was ready to accept and wanted me to go with him. Naturally, I was ready. We were married in 1946 in the early summertime, then headed off to Ocracoke Island.

We took sail from the mainland in kind of a small boat. It took us almost two hours to reach the island. All we saw was water everywhere! I began to really wonder where my husband was taking me. Thank God that all was well. We reached a Coast Guard Station on Ocracoke Island. We didn't see many cars because there were no paved roads, but the wild horses did well. The church was very nice, and the people were very friendly, loving, and kind.

The living quarters were a square two-room cottage with a thatched roof and no running water. We boiled rainwater and at times we had well water. To cook, we had an old burner-type stove. The only electricity was two light bulbs. There was no phone to use, although we had access to an outside telephone. There were grassy paths everywhere. We accepted our first abode as our mission field. I had no washer or dryer. We used tubs and a scrub board, and the wind did the drying. God was very faithful to us in every way.

We received five dollars every week. One week at Christmastime we received twenty dollars. We did not go hungry. There was plenty of fish to eat, which I did not like, but there were biscuits, eggs, chicken, and one grocery store. Praise God from who all blessings flow. I still hear from two island sisters at Christmas time every year.

My husband and I were not sent out to Ocracoke Island with any authorization for finances or anything for that matter. We trusted God completely. Proverbs 3:6 (KJV) says, *"In all thy ways acknowledge Him and He shall direct thy paths."* If we do this 100%, without a doubt God will never fail. God has never failed me, no matter what I have experienced in my walk with Him. Great is thy faithfulness! God is God!

In our later years, we were involved in the Teen Challenge ministry, the Training Center in Rehrersburg, PA, and Rochester, NY.

Our three sons were involved in the ministry as well. There are times I miss being in ministry, but I am in touch with my Lord and am being blessed daily.

God's Faithfulness to Me
Ruby Mayeski

One of my life verses is in Lamentations 3:23 (KJV)
"Thy mercies are new every morning.
GREAT IS THY FAITHFULNESS."

One of the ways God has shown His faithfulness to me is by providing mentors and helpers. My father died when I was six, and an elderly couple by the same last name as ours ("Sloan" – but not related) invited my mother and me to Sunday dinner each week for six years! It was such a loving comfort to us.

When I was ten years old, I knelt at the altar at a Methodist Church and accepted Jesus as my Savior. The pastor and his wife took me "under their wings" and encouraged me. Even at a young age, the pastor asked me to speak at a Good Friday Service. Then he urged me to get an "exhorter's license" and "pastor" a very small Methodist church nearby, which I did.

The church did much more for me than what I did for them. After serving there (from ages twelve to fourteen), my mother and stepfather moved to Quincy, Ill. My wonderful stepfather encouraged me to go to Asbury College where I enjoyed awesome chapel services and helped minister in churches in the Kentucky mountains.

God's faithfulness continued to uphold me as I became Director of Christian Education in a Methodist Church in VA, where the pastor and his wife mentored and encouraged me so much. After two years there, I married my high school sweetheart from Ill. The church gave us a beautiful Southern wedding.

The twelve ladies' circles each gave me a wedding shower. God showed me such love through this church, so I tried to pass it along to others.

God's faithfulness was again seen in the healing of our oldest daughter Rita when she was five years old. We were visiting my husband's parents when we noticed Rita's face was all distorted. We took her to Mom's doctor in Quincy, and she told us Rita had Bell's Palsy – paralysis on her face.

The doctor gave her a vitamin C shot. Since we had to leave to go back home, she taught me how to give the shot. I never did get proficient at this. When it was time for a shot, Rita would go into a frenzy, screaming and crying. After some time, I quit trying to give her a shot. We continued to pray for her healing. After three months, God healed her! Praise His Name!

The last thing I want to mention is His faithfulness to me at the time of the home-going of both of my wonderful husbands. When Richard died at age fifty-six, I felt so devastated and wondered how I could make it alone. The Holy Spirit and many friends helped me. Seven years later he gave me another wonderful husband, Anthony Mayeski.

The Lord gave us nineteen good years together, and he went "home" at age ninety-three. It's been over ten years now, and the Lord is still faithful. He is my rock and my strength!

Now at age ninety-three, I continue to seek God and believe Him for the healing of macular degeneration and deafness. He is so faithful in allowing me to walk in health and service to others each day.

Great Is His Faithfulness!

Stuck in The Miry Clay
Susan Snyder

"MOM!" My eleven-year-old son was calling. His plaintive voice came through the kitchen window to where I was preparing the evening meal. "I'm stuck," he said. He had been flying his kite, and it had come down in a field near our home. He was stuck all right in the mud of the recently plowed field.

"Pull your feet from your boots and scoot to the house," I called to him. Later I tried to get the boots loose, but they were held tightly in the mud. I dug the slimy muck from around the boots and pulled. As the suction was broken, they came free with a "slurp." At that moment the words of David's cry in Psalm 40:1-2 came to my mind. *"I waited patiently for the Lord, and he inclined unto me and heard my cry. He brought me up also out of a horrible pit, out of the miry clay, and set my feet upon a rock, and established my goings."* (KJV)

I had heard the phrase "miry clay" many times, but not until that day in our oozing cornfield did I realize what the words really meant. The sticky mud clung to my hands. Soap and water had to be generously applied before they were clean again.

My son had gone into the mud to get his brightly colored kite that had landed on the soft furrows. Without a second thought, he started across the field to get it.

Often, we may not be alert to the world's enticements calling us into temptation. The Bible tells us to *"Watch and pray, that ye enter not into temptation."* Matthew 26:41 (KJV).

Without prayer and watchfulness, we may find ourselves trapped in the slimy mud of sin. Only the love of Christ can loosen the grip of sin on our souls. It is the blood of Jesus alone that can wash our sins away.

Never again shall I read or hear the words "miry clay" without remembering the awful mud that trapped my son and stained my clothes. When I do remember, I shout in triumph with Paul,

"Thanks be to God, which gives us the victory through our Lord Jesus Christ." 1 Corinthians 15:57 (KJV)

Our One and Only Church
Rev. Francis Parmenteri

I was raised in a Pentecostal church and at the age of twelve, I gave my heart to Jesus. My wife Ruth and I attended the same church. She didn't really notice me until after I had joined the Navy. We had attended a CA Rally (Christ's Ambassadors) when she saw this handsome Navy man! The rest is history.

Ruth and I pastored our one and only church in Plymouth, PA. We started with five people and grew to 200. I thank God I was then able to pastor full-time.

We had attended a banquet for ministers who had supported the Oral Roberts healing services. At the close of the banquet, Rev. Roberts prayed and asked God to bless us. The next year our first son was born.

I have worked hard over the years and I stand upon these words from God's Word: *"And let us not be weary in well doing: for in due season we shall reap if we faint not."* Galatians 6:9 (KJV)

Healed from Tuberculosis
Rev. Harold Ladd

At the age of sixteen, I was released from a TB (Tuberculosis) sanatorium. It was at that time I accepted Jesus as my Lord and Savior. A few years later, after returning from WWII, I went to Zion Bible School for a visit. While there, I heard some students praying in the kitchen.

I was so hungry for God that I investigated it. That night I was baptized in the Holy Spirit and spoke in tongues for three hours.

I met my wife Dolores at Zion. We both belonged to a singing traveling group. We got well acquainted while ministering together. Eventually, we got married and were married for just over fifty years before the Lord took her home.

God, Our Guide, and Provider
Rev. Ted Graboski

One Sunday, I was sitting in a Catholic church service listening to the priest give his homily. He was reading Matthew 6:25-34 when I heard a voice explaining the meaning of the verses to me and speaking to me. Then I heard His question: "And what are you seeking?" That question shook me and so began my journey to find the answer to that question. God provided a job after school, introduced me to my wife, and gave me three daughters.

A few years later, my wife and I were looking for a house near where I had just taken a new job. My wife was home taking care of Joy-Anna, our firstborn. The housing market was tight. It was the 1980s and the interest rates were double-digit. We had begun attending a church in the area where I worked but we had not yet moved. The real estate agent was trying his best to find a house for us, and nothing happened for six months. Reluctantly, we stopped looking.

One day I was out to lunch near my plant and stopped at a gas station and asked the attendant if he knew of any homes for rent or sale in the area. He said no but said maybe I should talk to a mailman. I followed his advice and found a mailman who directed me to a house that was just being built. I went to see it and asked the workman still hanging drywall if I could come in and look around. As I stood in what would later be the living room, the Spirit said to me, "This is your house."

I called my real estate agent when I got back to my office and told him about the house. He checked it out and said it was a real deal. The prices of homes that my wife and I had looked at were in the $240,000 range. This house we purchased new had three bedrooms, two baths, a full basement and an acre of land for $69,900. It was well within our price range.

Three years later, God called me into ministry, and told us to sell the house and how much to ask for it. The house sold in half a day without an agent or even multi-listing it for the exact price we quoted.

Later, God provided jobs for me while I was a student. While walking on the university campus He told me to go to the university credit union and get a mortgage for the house we were planning to buy.

He also provided my wife and me with two cars. While singing in the church choir, He spoke to both Kathy and me to cut up our Sears credit card. When we arrived home, we compared what we heard Him say and did just that.

Being a Light Everywhere I Go
Priscilla Richmond

I first met my husband Rev. George Richmond in a small church in Markleysburg, PA.

The first church we pastored was in Prince Edward Island, Canada. After returning to Pennsylvania, we became Assemblies of God pastors. Our first A/G church was in Ellwood City. From there we went to Latrobe where we pastored for over seven years before George went home.

I have come to realize that God has a great sense of humor and I can do ALL things because He strengthens me. He is my Jehovah Jireh!

In 2013 I retired after working five years for FEMA. It was a blast and a wonderful opportunity to be a witness to co-workers and the survivors.

The most important thing we can ever do in this life is doing what we know God wants us to do. There's no greater joy than being in the center of God's will.

Honoring the Life and Ministry of Rev. Roger and Betty Pence
Patty Hamilton, Daughter

Ministry had long been a vital part of the life of Roger and Betty Pence. From the earliest days of their marriage, their involvement in their local church and the lives of others became a hallmark of their marriage as an outward expression of their love for the God they loved and served.

Early in their marriage, Roger was a lay minister in the local Baptist church. It was after Betty received the baptism of the Holy Spirit that Roger also embraced that Holy Spirit baptism. This major event in their spiritual lives led them to the Open Bible Church and later to the Assembly of God located in Freeport, PA.

While there they continued to be active in the church with Roger being called on to do fill-in pulpit ministry. While at Freeport, they felt a burden to establish a church closer to their home of Kittanning. This burden lead them, along with some close friends, to begin an Assembly of God Church in Adrian, PA.

Roger would become close friends with Rev. Asa Martin and Rev. Elmer Shinck. These two men became very instrumental in encouraging him to pursue credentials with the Assemblies of God.

He enrolled in the Berean courses being offered by the Assemblies of God. He went on to complete those courses and became an ordained minister with the Assemblies of God.

In 1965 Roger and Betty would receive a call from the Melcroft Assembly of God to become their pastor. Roger accepted the call to the church and would drive back and forth from Kittanning to Melcroft for approximately seven years. It was said that PPG had to shut down to move the Pences to Melcroft full time.

Rev. Pence and Betty witnessed the congregation grow until they had outgrown their facility. It was in 1971 that Roger challenged the congregation to step out in faith to build a new facility. Under that leadership, the members bought a parcel of ground along Route 711 and in March of 1971 construction began on a new building.

Rev. Pence became the "general contractor" overseeing the building program. Under his leadership, the church was built by volunteers from the congregation, community, and even family. Melcroft Assembly of God was completed in May of 1974. Within the following year, the church was paid off and the mortgage burned.

Under the ministry of the Pences, the church continued to grow, reaching many souls for the Kingdom of God. In 1991, following twenty-six years of ministry to the congregation at Melcroft, Roger and Betty decided to retire.

Rev. Pence would continue to do fill-in ministry for several years. After the death of his wife Betty Roger would spend time with his children and grandchildren until the time of his promotion into God's presence in August 2014.

We All Have a Mountain to Climb
Rev. Thomas Hamilton

As we walk through this life, we will face many mountains.
The mountains we encounter are never easy to climb.
Fact is, it is impossible to climb a smooth mountain.

Those who know anything about mountain climbing
know it's the rocks, the rough places, and the challenges
that help them to reach the top.

If the mountains were smooth, we would keep falling to the bottom again. It's the difficult situations in our lives that help us to grow and to keep climbing till we reach the top.

911 in Shanksville, PA
Rev. Sylvia Baker

(Sylvia pastored in Shanksville, PA during the 911 attack on our nation. She had the opportunity to "minister to millions of people around the world.")

September 11, 2001 – It was a day like any other day in Shanksville, PA. My neighbor and I took our usual early morning walk. We noted that everything seemed to be very quiet. Not much traffic on the roads and no animal "chatter" we were used to hearing.

We had to cut our sojourn short as a family was due to arrive and take me to the funeral home in a nearby town. All of a sudden, I heard a very large explosion and felt the house shake. I ran to the front door, feeling quite sure a truck had run into the front porch.

At about that time, my ride arrived and so we went to the funeral. While we were at the funeral, there was much whispering about what might have caused such a tremendous explosion. After the service, we could not go directly into Shanksville. Still not knowing what had happened, we took a very circuitous route through the cemetery.

Finally arriving home, my telephone started ringing "off the hook" about a plane crash in Shanksville. After some phone calls on my part, I learned that indeed a large jet plane had come down in a field not far from my house.

Since the church where I served as Pastor was Shanksville Assembly of God, it was the first church in the telephone number listings. My phone literally did not stop ringing until quite late into the evening. I had almost non-stop opportunities to talk and share with reporters and other interesting people from, literally, around the world.

For the next several weeks, a day never went by without calls about the September 11th disaster. I had the opportunity to talk and visit with many in my house or on the porch swing. One gentleman from England kept in touch with me for at least a year afterward.

As the Lord would open the door, I shared a scripture verse or two with those that were visiting with me. I prayed that those who prayed with me would have found their way to a walk with the Lord Jesus.

Thirty-Eight Years of Amazing Grace
Arlene Stubbs

It seems like only yesterday that Earl and I were earnestly praying to find a good Pentecostal church in our new city of ministry—Hyderabad, India—when God spoke to us: "You start one."

Although that had never been on our agenda, we simply obeyed and began holding meetings in our living room. We soon moved to a hotel conference room where our first service had fourteen people. When that space became too small, we moved to a car repair shop! Every Saturday the cars were moved out and our young people set up chairs for Sunday service. It became hallowed ground as people were saved and filled with the Holy Spirit.

When it was time to move again, we found a vacant old movie theater. It was a real hall with a stage and even a balcony. We were so excited, but it, too, was soon bulging at the seams. We literally extended the sides of our tent, building sheds outside the hall. Eventually almost three-fourths of our congregation (now running 6,000 in multiple services) were sitting outside watching the service on large screens. During those years, we searched for land on which to build our own church.

Then, the unthinkable happened. On the week we were preparing for our church's twenty-fifth anniversary, Earl suffered a heart attack and was gone within an hour. Then came the agonizing prayers of "Now What?"

Although I knew God wanted me back in Hyderabad, I was terrified of facing that daunting task alone. I gave the Lord all my heartfelt excuses: "I can't preach like Earl…how can I administrate that large congregation?"

So gently the Holy Spirit spoke to me: "Can you obey?"

"Yes, Lord!" Six weeks after Earl's burial, I was back in Hyderabad.

That was thirteen years ago, and God has continued to bless in ways we never thought possible. We found the land we had been praying and searching for. Through a series of miracles and the faithfulness of our congregation, we raised 12 million dollars to pay for that property.

When the land was paid for, we began construction on our very own church building. What a day of rejoicing in July 2018 when we dedicated that beautiful building to the glory of God. It was the fulfillment of a vision and a stepping stone into the new things God has in store for us.

This last year has brought new challenges as we cope with the effects of the Covid pandemic. We have had two periods of lockdown when no in-service meetings were allowed. During this time, we have never missed a Sunday service as our meetings go out on many forms of social media.

On July 11, 2021, we celebrated thirty-eight years of God's amazing grace. We have proved it once again that in every season, God is faithful! A very big thank you to our wonderful supporters from PennDel who have stood with us all these years. We could not have made it without you!

As of July 11, 2021:

- 19,620 conversions (99 in the past year)
- 3,002 baptized in water (28 in the past year)
- 2,127 baptized in the Spirit (5 filled this past year)
- 194 funerals
- 370 weddings
- 885 baby and child dedications
- In the past year, we had twenty-five funerals; many passed due to Covid-19.
- We had eighteen weddings and twenty-nine dedications.

To God Be the Glory!

"Who, Me Lord?"
Nurse/Midwife Edith Cochrane
Rev. Philip J Cochrane

She was so beautifully out of place, a white English Nurse/Midwife birthing babies and caring for lepers in the heart of Congo, Africa. It had been a long journey that started at a Wednesday night church meeting. Fifteen-year-old Edith Cochrane knelt at an altar and heard God call her to be a medical missionary to the Congo.

Lepers were outcasts. Once you received a diagnosis of "leprosy" you were thrown out of the village. Your family would never speak your name again. It would be a lonely, difficult, and miserable existence. You would be known as one of the "Dead People."

And now here she was at Biodi Clinic cleansing a leper's ulcerated feet. As she knelt bandaging his feet, the leper said, "Madamo, we know that you love us." Nurse Edith replied, "How do you know I love you?" The leper replied, "Because you touch us." God was starting to bring "dead" things to life.

The medical ministry grew as lepers were treated and healed. Nurse Edith Cochrane began to conduct nurse and midwife training. These former members of the "Dead People" now returned to bring life and healing to their family and their tribe. Once outcasts, they were now bringing the life-giving presence of God to their own people.

But soon on the horizon, dark, ominous clouds were forming. The church leaders came to the mission house to beg Nurse Edith and her family to escape from the approaching storm. Rebel soldiers, known as the "Simbas" were advancing on the Biodi Clinic. The Congolese pastors prayed with Phil and Edith Cochrane and urged them to leave quickly.

It was a hot, dusty journey. The VW Kombi van bounced over the heavily rutted dirt roads, rarely reaching more than 25 miles per hour. Headed for the border of Uganda, they prayed for safety. Suddenly, as they rounded a curve in the single-lane road, they ran right into a Simba convoy. AK47s, spears, and machetes were pointed at the Kombi van. They were prisoners of war.

They were now forced to travel with the Simba convoy. Simba soldiers rode inside the van to make sure that the Cochranes and their four children did not escape. The convoy stopped every few miles so that the Simba rebels could terrorize the villagers, hunt for government officials, and plunder homes and businesses.

At one of these stops, Nurse Cochrane gathered her infant daughter, Ruth, and went to stand in front of the rebel commander. She addressed him respectfully and then said, "I have healed your Mothers and Fathers, I have birthed your sons and your daughters, and now my baby is about to die. I have no more milk for her.

Please let us travel to the mission station at Aba so that we can get some milk for the baby. But if this baby dies, her blood will be on your head."

The commander quickly asked for paper and a pen. He wrote out a travel document authorizing free travel through all rebel-held land….and in a minute, we were suddenly free!

We would be captured a second time. This story, and many more, are in the book written by Nurse Cochrane called, "Who Me Lord."

This book is available as a free eBook download. Just go to: **CongoNurseScholarshipProject.org**

You can also follow Nurse Cochrane's continuing work in Congo by going to:
facebook.com/groups/congonurse

No More Regrets
Vivian Dippold

Preface: As a Believer, I expect miracles. I wait for those good things to happen. I definitely know that His promises are true, and that's how I approached my life's experiences. I know He traveled beside me in my dark moments of humanness. There is no doubt that He is my Guide, the Way Maker, and my Shepherd. Therefore, within this framework, there should have been no regrets. I wish that was the case.

April 2021 - I admire those who say they have no regrets in their lives. There is nothing they would change. Looking back, they say there is nothing to ponder with remorse. I only wish I could be that fortunate.

It has been over three years since my life partner, best friend, husband and the father of our children left this earth for a place far better and far more beautiful. I miss him. I miss him every day.

It was a very long, arduous journey as we faced the turbulence of ten long years of battling three different types of cancer. Each time we expected it to disappear by God's miracle-working power. Instead of tremendous victories, we often struggled with the cancer appearing in a different form, a different place.

With mountain tops of good results, there were avalanches of desperation when the doctors would shake their heads, giving negative reports. Unfortunately, this is where much of my regret reared its ugly head.

It was here, after days and months of no relief, I, unfortunately, became impatient. That's one huge regret. I didn't know the extent of his pain, his discomfort, or the difficulty he faced in general. During the day he would sit, hand to his chin, just staring and waiting.

My next regret was not asking his thoughts or pushing him to talk to me, to explain to me more in-depth what was going on. I regret not listening more closely or pleading more earnestly with the doctors for greater insight into what we were facing. We were just waiting for change to come.

There were times I didn't fully understand his level of distress. He often bore it silently. I couldn't feel the pain or the constant nagging of damaged nerve endings. There were times his face registered discomfort. Some nights he would toss and turn, looking for and waiting for relief. Then, often through tears and my own anxiety, I would lay with my head on his thinning chest and say, "I'm sorry. I just don't know what to do."

I acknowledge those regrets, but here's one thing I don't regret.
- From the time we were joined as husband and wife to the time beside his hospital bed.
- I don't regret the times of prayer and reaching and clasping each other's hands.

- I don't regret following God's plan for our lives as we served in forty-nine years of various forms of ministry.
- I don't regret always seeking God's mercy and guidance as we raised four children in those sometimes difficult fifty-one years that we were together.
- I don't regret loving him for better or worse and being thankful for richer and poorer years.

God was always present. He took us through those deep valleys. Yet, I don't regret the journey. It was only God's provision and care that sustained the walk.

As I look ahead, the regret now turns to a smile because I know he is pain-free and has joined other family and friends marching, singing and dancing down the Heavenly streets now called Home.

At this point, if he does see me in the earthly domain (Okay, I know that's stretching theology!), I'm sure he's saying, "It's okay. I'm okay. As a matter of fact, I've never been better. Please, no more regrets."